Piano Book for Adult Beginners

Teach Yourself How to Play Famous Piano Songs, Read Music, Theory & Technique

No Music Reading Required!

Damon Ferrante

Book & Streaming Video Lessons

Introduction: How the Book & Videos Work

As a piano professor and piano teacher for over twenty five years, I have wanted to help beginner piano students succeed in playing famous and beautiful music. In the past, beginner piano books have taken a dull and uninspiring approach. Most of the time these books just throw together songs and techniques in a random, boring, and confusing way; sometimes these books are no better than blurry photocopies.

This book and video course takes a new and innovative approach!

The Piano Book for Adult Beginners makes learning famous piano pieces fun, easy, interactive, and engaging. The book and streaming videos follow a step-by-step lesson format for learning some of the most famous music. Pieces you have always dreamt about playing on the piano for yourself and for your family and friends!

In the *Piano Book for Adult Beginners,* each lesson builds on the previous one in a clear and easy-to-understand manner. No music reading is necessary. I walk you through how to play these wonderful pieces, starting with very easy music, at the beginning of the book, and advancing, little by little, as you master new repertoire and techniques. As you are able to play these new pieces, you will also greatly improve your abilities on the piano! Along the way, you will learn to read music, play chords and scales, learn rhythms, techniques, and music theory, as well.

If you have always wanted to play the piano, then, this book is for you. Let's get started on this exciting musical journey!

The Videos

This symbol means that there is a video lesson that corresponds to the material presented on the lesson page. These video lessons cover the concepts presented and also give instruction and tips on how to play certain famous pieces from the book.

To access the video lessons, go to steeplechasemusic.com and click on the link at the top of the page for Piano Books. Then, from the Piano Books webpage, click on the image for this book, "Piano Book for Adult Beginners". On the webpage for the *Piano Book for Adult Beginners*, you will see a link to Video Lessons. Click that link for the Video Lessons webpage for this book. The video lessons are free and there is no limit on the number of times you may watch them.

Here is a list of some of the <u>Great</u> <u>Piano</u> <u>Music</u> that you will learn in this book:

- *Für Elise* by Beethoven
- *The Entertainer* by Scott Joplin
- *Amazing Grace*
- Pachelbel's *Canon*
- *House of the Rising Sun*
- *Scarborough Fair*
- *Turkish Rondo* by Mozart
- *Shenandoah*
- *Happy Birthday*
- *Danny Boy*
- *Kum-Bah-Yah*
- *Jingle Bells*
- J.S. Bach's *Prelude in C Major*
- *Home on the Range*
- *This Little Light of Mine*
- *Hall of the Mountain King* by Grieg
- *Take Me Out to the Ballgame*
- *Red River Valley*
- *Silent Night*
- *New World Symphony Theme*
- *When the Saints Go Marching In*
- *Greensleeves*
- *Aura Lee*
- *Brahms' Famous Lullaby*
- *Simple Gifts*
- And Many More Songs and Pieces!

You will also learn how to read music, play with both hands at the same time, play chords and scales, as well as many more exciting piano techniques!

Table of Contents

Section 1: Introduction & Basic Music Concepts

Page:

1. Introduction & Review of Basic Music Concepts
2. Hand Position & Finger Numbers
3. Finding Middle C & Good Posture at the Piano
4. Learning the Notes on the Keyboard
5. Three-Note Songs Using the Right Hand
6. More Three-Note Songs Using the Right Hand
7. An Overview of Counting & Measures
8. Counting along with Three-Note Songs in the Right Hand
9. The Melody for *Jingle Bells*
10. Beethoven's *Ode to Joy*
11. Three-Note Songs Using the Left Hand
12. More Three-Note Songs Using the Left Hand
13. An Overview of Time Signatures
14. Counting along with Three-Note Songs Using the Left Hand
15. Five-Note Songs for the Left Hand
16. More Five-Note Songs for the Left Hand
17. Song for Both Hands: *Yankee Doodle*
18. Song for Both Hands: *Twinkle, Twinkle, Little Star*
19. Song for Both Hands: *Take Me Out to the Ballgame*
20. Music Theory: What are Intervals?
21. Song for Both Hands at the Same Time: *Fanfare*
22. Song for Both Hands at the Same Time: *Love Somebody*
23. Songs for Both Hands at the Same Time: *Ode to Joy* (Advanced)
24. Upbeats & *When the Saints Go Marching In*
25. Whole Notes, Half Notes & Quarter Notes
26. Songs with Half Notes & Quarter Notes
27. Five-Note Songs with Half Notes & Quarter Notes for Right Hand
28. Five-Note Songs with Whole Notes, Half Notes & Quarter Notes
29. Five-Note Songs with Half Notes & Quarter Notes for Left Hand
30. More Five-Note Songs for the Left Hand
31. Reading Music: Notes of the Treble Clef
32. Reading Music: Treble Clef Exercises
33. Reading Music: More Treble Clef Exercises
34. Overview: The Treble Clef Lines
35. Overview: The Treble Clef Spaces
36. *Kum-Bah-Yah*
37. Reading Music: Notes of the Bass Clef
38. Reading Music: Bass Clef Exercises
39. Reading Music: More Bass Clef Exercises

40. Overview: The Bass Clef Lines
41. Overview: The Bass Clef Spaces
42. Reading Music: Bass Clef Exercises
44. Pachelbel's *Canon* & Grieg's *Hall of the Mountain King* Melodies
45. Overview: The Grand Staff

Section 2: Famous Songs & Pieces of Music

47. Famous Songs & Pieces of Music
49. *Simple Gifts*
51. *Amazing Grace* & Counting in 3/4 Time
52. *Jingle Bells*
54. *Michael, Row the Boat Ashore*
55. *In May*
56. *Danny Boy*
58. Music Theory: What are Sharps & Flats?
60. *Scarborough Fair*
61. Overview of Chords
65. *Red River Valley* & *Aura Lee*
66. *Ode to Joy* (Chord Version)
67. *Jazz Dance*
68. *House of the Rising Sun*
70. Music Theory: Overview of Dynamics
71. *Simple Gifts* & Overview of Eighth Notes
75. *Happy Birthday*
77. Brahms' *Lullaby* & Chord Accompaniment
79. *Shenandoah* & *Hineh Ma Tov*
80. *Home on the Range*
81. *This Little Light of Mine*
82. *Greensleeves*
85. J.S. Bach's *Prelude in C Major*
88. Music Theory: What is a Scale?
90. Major Scales: C, G & D
93. Dvořák's *New World Symphony Theme* & Dotted Rhythms
95. *Silent Night*
96. Mozart's *Turkish Rondo*
98. Grieg's *Hall of the Mountain King*
102. Pachelbel's *Canon*
105. *The Entertainer* by Scott Joplin
106. *Für Elise* by Beethoven
108. About the Author
109. Additional Reading
111. Becoming the Pianist of Your Dreams!

Table of Contents for the Video Lessons

1: Hand Position & Finger Numbers
2: An Overview of Counting & Measures
3: An Overview of Time Signatures
4: Music Theory: What are Intervals?
5: Whole Notes, Half Notes & Quarter Notes
6: The Treble Clef
7: The Bass Clef
8: The Grand Staff
9: How to Play *Simple Gifts*
10: How to Play *Amazing Grace*
11: Music Theory: What are Sharps & Flats?
12: Easy Piano Chords
13: How to Play Beethoven's *Ode to Joy*
14: How to Play Um-Pah Chords
15: How to Play Bach's *C Major Prelude*
16: Music Theory: How to Play Scales on the Piano, Part 1
17: Music Theory: How to Play Scales on the Piano, Part 2 (Thumb Under)
18: Music Theory: What are Minor Scales?
19: How to Play Pachelbel's *Canon*
20: How to Play Beethoven's *Für Elise*

Important!

To access the video lessons, go to steeplechasemusic.com and click on the link at the top of the page for Piano Books. Then, from the Piano Books webpage, click on the image for this book, "Piano Book for Adult Beginners". On the webpage for the "Piano Book for Adult Beginners", you will see a link to Video Lessons. Click that link for the Video Lessons webpage for this book. The video lessons are free and there is no limit on the number of times you may watch them.

Getting Started

The inspiration for this book came from helping people who have dreamt of playing the piano, but who haven't known where to begin. Over the last few decades of playing and teaching the piano, I have picked up a few helpful pointers that I would like to share with you at the beginning of the book:

1. One of the most important aspects for learning an instrument is cultivating a positive attitude. If you approach learning the piano with a happy, fun-loving spirit, your mind and body will be much more receptive to learning new ideas. Having a can-do, positive outlook will not only make the process of learning more fun, but it has been proven to speed up the process of improving. So, you should always approach your piano playing as an exciting and rewarding activity of your day.

2. Another important aspect of playing the piano is forming good practice habits. Learning the piano is a fun and creative endeavor; if you develop good practice habits you will make rapid progress with your playing. This will require a little bit of focus and a proactive attitude on your part. However, it will make a big difference for you.

   Ideally, you should strive to practice around five to seven times per week (once per day) for about 20 to 40 minutes. If you have more time, that's great. However, it's best to spend your time practicing well (in an organized manner), rather than just spending a lot of time practicing. Along these lines, one of the most important facets of learning to play the piano is having some continuity in your practice routine. So, even on days that you are extremely busy, try to take 10-15 minutes to work on your piano playing. As best as you can, try to avoid missing more than three days of practicing in a row.

3. Have patience and a longterm perspective: You are embarking on a grand and lifelong adventure in music. Through this journey, you will discover new perspectives on sound, communication, friendship, success, coordination, self confidence, concentration, memory, and determination. For the most part, this learning will be a step-by-step process, where your ability and understanding of music will move ahead at a gradual pace. At other times, your progress may suddenly leap ahead to another level in a flash of inspiration.

Whatever your goals in music may be, it's best to cultivate an attitude that music is a lifelong journey and process of creating and developing. As an artist, you should continue to explore and develop your musical voice. Life will take you along different paths and these will be reflected in your music making. Enjoy this adventure, especially if you are just beginning. You are like some explorer stepping onto the deck of your ship heading out from your land's port to find yet-unexplored, new places. Enjoy the journey!

4. Lastly, a lot of beginning musicians overlook the importance of practicing with a metronome. A metronome is a mechanical or electronic device that keeps a steady beat. You can change the speed of the beats, which in music is called the "tempo", on all metronomes to allow for slower or faster pulses of rhythm.

As soon as possible, you should incorporate a metronome into your practicing for these piano pieces. This will help build and solidify your internal rhythm.

You can find a number of free or inexpensive metronome apps online. These will work on your computer, tablet, and smartphone. There are also a wide assortment of digital metronomes that you can purchase. Many of these can be found online or at your local music store for around ten dollars.

Damon Ferrante

GOOD NEWS: BONUS LESSONS!

This edition of *The Piano Book for Adult Beginners* includes free, bonus lessons.

1. Go to the Home Page of SteeplechaseMusic.com.

2. At the top of the Home Page, you will see a link for <u>Piano Books</u>.

3. Follow the link to the <u>Piano Books</u> webpage.

4. Then, click on the <u>Cover / Link</u> for *The Piano Book for Adult Beginners.*

5. Once you are on the webpage for *The Piano Book for Adult Beginners*, click on the link bonus lessons.

Steeplechase Music Books

Also by Damon Ferrante

Piano Scales, Chords & Arpeggios Lessons with Elements of Basic Music Theory: Fun, Step-By-Step Guide for Beginner to Advanced Levels (Book & Videos)

Beginner Classical Piano Music: Teach Yourself How to Play Famous Piano Pieces by Bach, Mozart, Beethoven & the Great Composers (Book, Streaming Videos & MP3 Audio)

Guitar Adventures: Fun, Step-By-Step Guide to Beginner Guitar for Kids (Book & Videos)

Guitar Scales Handbook: A Step-By-Step, 100-Lesson Guide to Scales, Music Theory, and Fretboard Theory (Book & Videos)

Beginner Rock Guitar Lessons: Instruction Guide (Book & Videos)

Ultimate Guitar Chords, Scales & Arpeggios Handbook: 240-Lesson, Step-By-Step Guitar Guide, Beginner to Advanced Levels (Book & Videos)

The Piano Book for Adult Beginners: Teach Yourself How to Play Famous Piano Songs, Read Music, Theory & Technique (Book & Streaming Video Lessons)

by Damon Ferrante

For additional information about music books, recordings, and concerts, please visit the Steeplechase website: www.steeplechasemusic.com

steeplechase
arts & productions

ISBN-13: 978-0692926437 (Steeplechase Arts)
ISBN-10: 0692926437

Section 1:
Introduction &
Basic Music
Concepts

Section 1: Introduction and Review of Basic Music Concepts

Section 1 of this book serves as a review of basic music and piano concepts or as an introduction to these ideas for readers who are just beginning to play the piano for the first time. The focus of Section 1 is to present some of these beginner-level piano fundamentals, like the finger numbers, names of the notes, the treble and bass clefs, counting and rhythm, and playing with both hands. If you have some experience playing the piano already and can read music, you may want to glance over the lessons in this section as a brief review, before starting on Section 2: Famous Songs & Pieces. If you are new to the piano or are not familiar with these concepts, take your time with the lessons in Section 1; they will provide you with a good foundation for playing the music in Section 2.

Although there are some pieces of music in Section 1, the primary goal for this section is to introduce you to basic music and piano concepts or refresh your memory about them, if you are resuming your piano studies. Interspersed throughout Section 1, there are excerpts of famous pieces for the right hand, left hand, or hands together. There are also exercises to help you practice rhythm, counting, learning the notes on the keyboard, and playing with both hands at the same time. Some of the pieces included in Section 1 are easier versions of pieces that will also appear in Section 2.

The Video Lessons:

Check out video

This symbol means that there is a video lesson that corresponds to the material presented on the lesson page. These video lessons cover the concepts presented and also give tips on how to play certain famous pieces from the book.

To access the video lessons, go to steeplechasemusic.com and click on the link at the top of the page for Piano Books. Then, from the Piano Books webpage, click on the image for this book, "The Beginner Piano Book". On the webpage for *The Beginner Piano Book*, you will see a link to Video Lessons. Click that link for the Video Lessons webpage for this book. The video lessons are free and there is no limit on the number of times you may watch them.

Hand Position & Finger Numbers

Check out video 1

- To create a good hand position for piano playing is easy. With both hands, imagine that you are holding an apple (with your palms facing upward and your fingers curved). Then, turn your palms to the floor and keep your fingers curved. **See Video Lesson 1**
- For piano playing, our fingers are given numbers. The numbers are the same for both hands. **See Video Lesson 1**

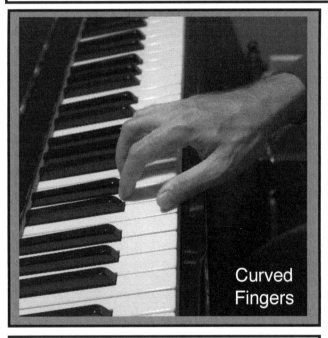

Curved Fingers

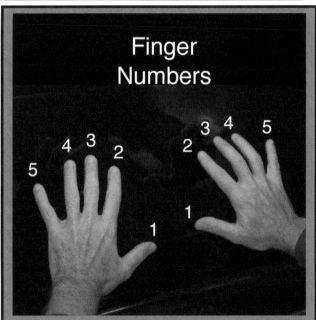

Finger Numbers

- RH stands for Right Hand.
- LH stands for Left Hand.

Finger Numbers
- Thumb = Finger #1
- Pointer = Finger #2
- Middle = Finger #3
- Ring = Finger #4
- Pinky = Finger #5

The finger numbers are the same for both hands. For example, the thumb is finger #1 in both the right hand and left hand and the pinky is finger #5 in both hands.

For Video Lesson 1, go to www.steeplechasemusic.com.

Finding Middle C
& Good Posture at the Piano

Check out video 1

- On the piano keyboard, you might notice that there are 2 sets of keys: black and white keys. The black keys are in groups of 2 and 3 keys.
- If you look near the middle of the piano keyboard, you will see a set of 2 black keys. The White key, directly to the left of this set of 2 Black Keys (near the middle of the piano keyboard) is called "Middle C".
- Middle C is an important reference note on the piano. We will be playing it in many of our songs and pieces later in this book.
- For some help in locating Middle C on the piano, **See Video Lesson 1.**

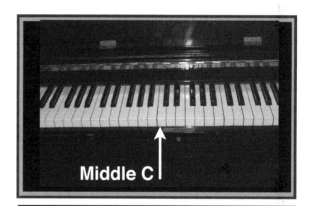

Middle C

From the beginning of your piano playing, it is important to practice good posture: keep your back straight and your arms and shoulders relaxed.

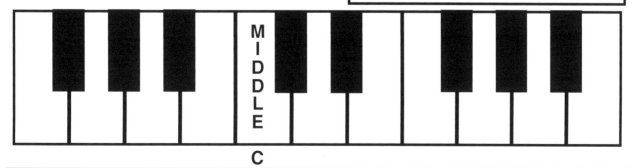

MIDDLE C

Exercises:

- Try Locating Middle C with Finger #1 (Thumb) of your Right Hand (RH)
- Try Locating Middle C with Finger #1 (Thumb) of your Left Hand (LH)

Learning the Notes of the Keyboard

- The White Keys on the piano follow an alphabetic pattern that goes from A to G. In other words, this is the pattern: A, B, C, D, E, F, G.
- The pattern starts at the bottom (low bass notes) of the piano keyboard and repeats many times as the notes go upward and get higher in pitch ("sound").
- With your RH ("Right Hand") Index Finger, find the "A" key just 2 keys below MIddle C (See the Chart below). Move your Index Finger up (to the right) one key at a time. Try saying the letters as you press down each key.

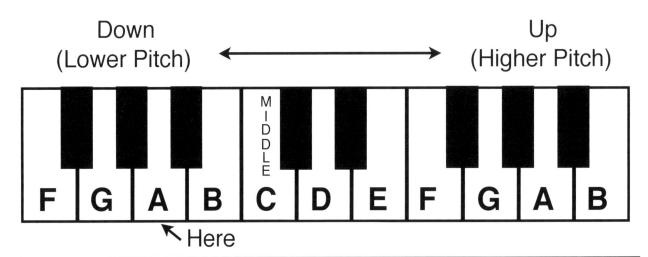

Down (Lower Pitch) ← → Up (Higher Pitch)

- It is a good idea to associate each key with some object and imagine the object on top of the key. This will help you remember the name and location of each key.
- For this exercise, let's image that the piano keyboard is a table with food on it. The food, on this imagined table, will be placed in a set order going from left to right (See the chart below). Find the key "A" below Middle C and name the foods as you move upward (right). When you get to the second key "A", the pattern will repeat. Repeat this exercise.

White Keys Exercise: A= Apple, B= Bread, C= Cheese, D= Dessert, E= Eggs, F= Fish, G= Grapes

Exercises:
- Try Locating Middle C with Finger #1 (Thumb) of your Right Hand (RH)
- Try Locating Middle C with Finger #1 (Thumb) of your Left Hand (LH)
- Try Locating D with Finger #2 (Pointer Finger) of your Right Hand (RH)
- Try Locating E with Finger #3 (Middle Finger) of your Right Hand (RH)
- Try Locating G with Finger #5 (Pinky Finger) of your Right Hand (RH)

Three-Note Songs, Using the Right Hand ("RH")

- Try these songs, which use the notes C, D, and E in the right hand ("RH").
- In your right hand, use your thumb for Middle C, use your pointer for D, and use your middle Finger for E on the piano keyboard.
- Take a look at the keyboard chart and photo below and practice each song five to ten times.
- As an extra bonus, try saying the letter names aloud as you play each song. This will help you associate the note name with the key and finger number.

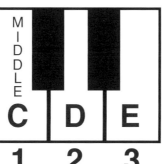

Notes:
Finger Numbers:

C, D, and E in the Right Hand

Springtime

RH: 1 1 1 1 | 2 2 2 2 | 3 3 3 3 | 2 2 1 1 ‖
    C C C C | D D D D | E E E E | D D C C ‖

Dancing

RH: 1 1 2 2 | 1 1 3 3 | 1 1 2 2 | 1 1 1 1 ‖
    C C D D | C C E E | C C D D | C C C C ‖

More Three-Note Songs, Using the Right Hand

Try these songs, which also use the notes C, D, and E in the right hand ("RH").

RH

Notes: C D E
Finger Numbers: 1 2 3

Try saying the notes aloud as you play each song.

The double lines (called the "Double Bar") indicate the end of a song or piece.

Jazz Dance

RH: 2 2 1 1 | 2 2 3 3 | 2 2 1 2 | 2 2 1 2 ‖
     D D C C | D D E E | D D C D | D D C D

Blue Sky

RH: 3 2 3 1 | 2 2 2 2 | 3 2 3 1 | 2 2 1 1 ‖
     E D E C | D D D D | E D E C | D D C C

Sunny Afternoon

RH: 1 1 3 3 | 2 2 3 3 | 1 1 3 3 | 2 2 1 1 ‖
     C C E E | D D E E | C C E E | D D C C

An Overview of Counting & Measures

- Music is composed of groups of beats called measures.
- Measures are set off by vertical lines, called bar lines.
- Measures most commonly contain 2, 3, or 4 beats.
- Below, are examples of sets of four measures in 4/4 time.
- In 4/4 time, you will count 4 beats for each measure.
  In other words, you will count: 1234, 1234, 1234, 1234.
- Count aloud and clap the beats for the exercises below.

Check out video 2

Example 1:

| 1 2 3 4 | 1 2 3 4 | 1 2 3 4 | 1 2 3 4 ‖

Example 2:
Try Clapping on the X: On the First Beat.

| 1 2 3 4 | 1 2 3 4 | 1 2 3 4 | 1 2 3 4 ‖
| X | X | X | X

Example 3:
Try Clapping on the X: On the First and Third Beats.

| 1 2 3 4 | 1 2 3 4 | 1 2 3 4 | 1 2 3 4 ‖
| X   X | X   X | X   X | X   X

Example 4:
Try Clapping on the X: On the Second Beat.

| 1 2 3 4 | 1 2 3 4 | 1 2 3 4 | 1 2 3 4 ‖
| X | X | X | X

Counting along with Three-Note Songs in the Right Hand

- Try counting aloud (1234) for each measure, while playing these songs.

- The songs use the notes C, D, and E in the right hand ("RH"):
  Fingers 1, 2, and 3 (Thumb, Pointer, and Middle). *Have fun!*

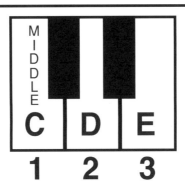

RH

Notes:

Finger Numbers:

C D E

1 2 3

The Numbers in these songs are for the <u>Beats</u>, <u>not</u> the Finger Numbers.

Summer Rock

Beats: **1 2 3 4** | **1 2 3 4** | **1 2 3 4** | **1 2 3 4**

D D C D | D D C D | E E D D | E E D D

A Short Walk

Beats: **1 2 3 4** | **1 2 3 4** | **1 2 3 4** | **1 2 3 4**

C C C C | D D D D | E E D D | C C C C

When's Dessert?

Beats: **1 2 3 4** | **1 2 3 4** | **1 2 3 4** | **1 2 3 4**

E D C C | D D E E | D D C D | E D C C

Jingle Bells & Mary's Lamb, More Right-Hand Songs

- Let's add 2 new notes for the right hand ("RH"): F and G.
- F will be played with the 4th finger (Ring Finger).
- G will be played with the 5th finger (Pinky Finger).
- Let's try this out with excerpt's from two classics.

RH

Notes: C D E F G

Finger Numbers: 1 2 3 4 5

The numbers here are for <u>beats</u>, not fingers. When there is a blank space, don't play for that beat or beats.

⟵ New Notes

Mary's Little Lamb

Beats:	1	2	3	4		1	2	3	4		1	2	3	4		1	2	3	4	
	E	D	C	D		E	E	E			D	D	D			E	G	G		
	Ma-	ry	had	a		lit-	tle	lamb,			lit-	tle	lamb,			lit-	tle	lamb.		

Jingle Bells

Beats:	1	2	3	4		1	2	3	4		1	2	3	4		1	2	3	4	
	E	E	E			E	E	E			E	G	C	D		E				
	Jin-	gle	Bells,			Jin-	gle	Bells,			Jin-	gle	all	the		way.				

Beats:	1	2	3	4		1	2	3	4		1	2	3	4		1	2	3	4	
	F	F	F	F		F	E	E	E		E	D	D	E		D		G		
	Oh!	What	fun	it		is	to	ride	in		a	one-horse	open			sleigh!		Hey!		

More Right-Hand, Five-Note Songs: Ode to Joy

- Here are a few more songs that use the five fingers of the right hand.
- Remember to find Middle C with the Thumb of your right hand (RH).
- We will learn a more advanced version of Beethoven's *Ode to Joy,* later in this book.

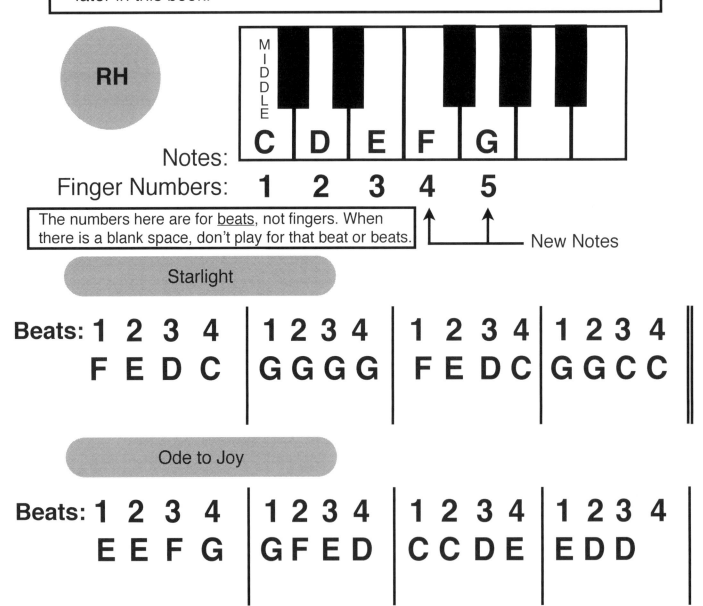

RH

Notes: C D E F G
Finger Numbers: 1 2 3 4 5

The numbers here are for <u>beats</u>, not fingers. When there is a blank space, don't play for that beat or beats.

New Notes

Starlight

Beats:	1	2	3	4		1	2	3	4		1	2	3	4		1	2	3	4	
	F	E	D	C		G	G	G	G		F	E	D	C		G	G	C	C	

Ode to Joy

Beats:	1	2	3	4		1	2	3	4		1	2	3	4		1	2	3	4	
	E	E	F	G		G	F	E	D		C	C	D	E		E	D	D		

Beats:	1	2	3	4		1	2	3	4		1	2	3	4		1	2	3	4	
	E	E	F	G		G	F	E	D		C	C	D	E		D	C	C		

Three-Note Songs, Using the Left Hand ("LH")

- Try these songs, which use the notes A, B, and Middle C in the left hand.

- In your left hand, use Thumb for Middle C, use Pointer for B, and use Middle Finger for A.

- Take a look at the keyboard chart and photo below and practice each song five to ten times.

- As an extra bonus, try saying the letter names aloud as you play each song. This will help you associate the note name with the key and finger number.

LH

Notes: **A B C** (MIDDLE)

Finger Numbers: **3 2 1**

The numbers here are for <u>fingers</u>, not beats.

A, B, and C in the Left Hand

In Winter

LH: **1 1 2 3** | **1 1 2 3** | **2 2 3 3** | **2 2 3 3** ‖
  C C B A | **C C B A** | **B B A A** | **B B A A**

A Mystery

LH: **3 2 1 2** | **3 2 1 2** | **1 1 3 3** | **1 2 3 3** ‖
  A B C B | **A B C B** | **C C A A** | **C B A A**

11

More Three-Note Songs
Using the Left Hand

Try these songs, which also use the notes A, B, and C in the Left hand ("LH").

LH

Notes: **A** **B** **C**

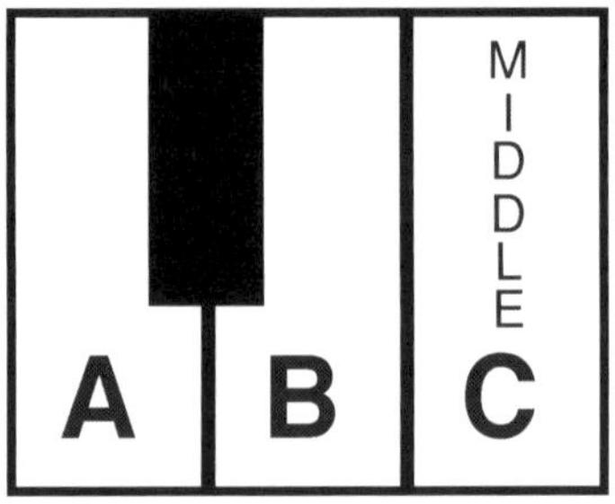

Finger Numbers: **3** **2** **1**

Try saying the notes aloud as you play each song.

The numbers here are for <u>fingers</u>, not beats.

Moments

LH: **2 3 2 3** | **1 1 1 1** | **2 3 2 3** | **1 1 3 3** ‖
B A B A | **C C C C** | **B A B A** | **C C A A**

Clouds

LH: **1 3 2 1** | **1 3 2 1** | **2 2 3 3** | **1 2 3 3** ‖
C A B C | **C A B C** | **B B A A** | **C B A A**

The Storm

LH: **1 3 1 3** | **2 3 2 3** | **1 3 1 3** | **2 2 3 3** ‖
C A C A | **B A B A** | **C A C A** | **B B A A**

An Overview of Time Signatures

- Measures are composed of groups of beats called Time Signatures or Meter (both terms mean the same thing and are interchangeable).
- The most common Time Signatures (or "meters") are groups of 2, 3, or 4 beats per measure: 2/4, 3/4, and 4/4 Time Signatures.
- 2/4 Time Signature groups the notes into measures of 2 beats. Count: "One, Two" for each measure.
- 3/4 Time Signature groups the notes into measures of 3 beats. Count: "One, Two, Three" for each measure.
- 4/4 Time Signature groups the notes into measures of 4 beats. Count: "One, Two, Three, Four" for each measure.
- Below, are examples of sets of four measures in 2/4, 3/4, and 4/4.
- Count aloud and clap on the first beat for the exercises below.

Check out video 3

Example 1: 2/4 Time Signature
Try Clapping on the X: On the First Beat.

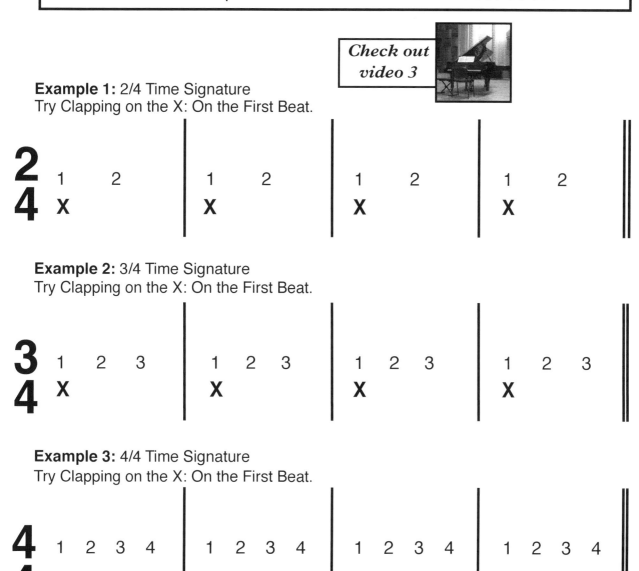

Example 2: 3/4 Time Signature
Try Clapping on the X: On the First Beat.

Example 3: 4/4 Time Signature
Try Clapping on the X: On the First Beat.

Counting along with Three-Note Songs Using the Left Hand in 3/4 Time

• Try counting aloud (123) for each measure, while playing these songs. The songs are all in 3/4 Time Signatures (which can also be called "3/4 Time").

• The songs use the notes A, B, and C in the left hand: Fingers 3, 2, and 1.

LH

Notes: A B C (MIDDLE)
Finger Numbers: 3 2 1

*The Numbers in these songs are for the Beats, not the Finger Numbers.

Waltz in A Minor

Beats:

3	1	2	3	1	2	3	1	2	3	1	2	3
4	C	A	A	C	A	A	B	A	A	C	A	A

Falling Leaves

Beats:

3	1	2	3	1	2	3	1	2	3	1	2	3
4	A	B	C	A	B	C	B	A	B	C	B	A

A Memory

Beats:

3	1	2	3	1	2	3	1	2	3	1	2	3
4	C	B	A	C	C	C	B	B	B	C	B	A

Five-Note Songs
for the Left Hand (LH)

- Let's add 2 new notes for the left hand ("LH"): F and G.
- F will be played with the 5th finger (Pinky Finger).
- G will be played with the 4th finger (Ring Finger).

LH

Notes: | F | G | A | B | C |

Finger Numbers: 5 4 3 2 1

New Notes

- These 2 songs are in 3/4 time (or "time signature").
- Remember to count "One, Two, Three" for each measure.
- The numbers here are for the <u>beats</u>, not the fingers.

Sunny Day

Beats:

3
4

| 1 | 2 | 3 | 1 | 2 | 3 | 1 | 2 | 3 | 1 | 2 | 3 |
| C | A | F | C | A | F | G | G | C | C | A | F |

Waves

Beats:

3
4

| 1 | 2 | 3 | 1 | 2 | 3 | 1 | 2 | 3 | 1 | 2 | 3 |
| F | G | A | F | A | C | F | G | A | C | A | F |

More Five-Note Songs for the Left Hand (LH)

- Here are a few more songs that use the five fingers of the left hand.
- Remember to find Middle C with the Thumb of your left hand (LH).

LH

Notes: F G A B C

Finger Numbers: 5 4 3 2 1

These 2 songs are in 4/4 time. Remember to count four beats for each measure. The numbers here are for <u>beats</u>, not fingers.

Mountain View

Beats:

1 2 3 4	1 2 3 4	1 2 3 4	1 2 3 4
F G A G	C C G G	F G A G	C B C C

(time signature 4/4)

Weekend Day Trip

Beats:

1 2 3 4	1 2 3 4	1 2 3 4	1 2 3 4
C G F G	C G F G	A A C C	G G G G

(time signature 4/4)

1 2 3 4	1 2 3 4	1 2 3 4	1 2 3 4
C G F G	C G F G	A A C C	G F F F

Songs for Both Hands: Yankee Doodle

> • Let's add 2 notes: G in the Left Hand and F in the Right Hand.
> • Both of these new notes will be played with the Ring Fingers.

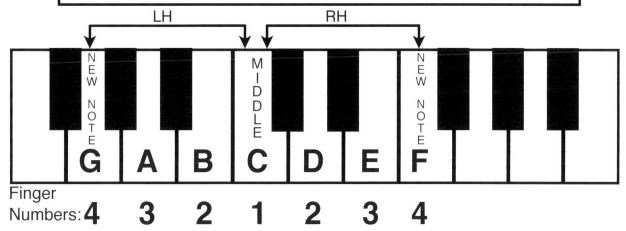

Finger Numbers: **4 3 2 1 2 3 4**

Both Thumbs (RH and LH) share Middle C.

Yankee Doodle

$\frac{4}{4}$

RH:	C	C	D	E	C	E	D		C	C	D	E	C			
Beats:	1	2	3	4	1	2	3	4	1	2	3	4	1	2	3	4
LH:															B	

RH:	C	C	D	E	F	E	D	C					C		C	
Beats:	1	2	3	4	1	2	3	4	1	2	3	4	1	2	3	4
LH:									B	G	A	B				

March

$\frac{4}{4}$

RH:	C		C				C		C		C				C	C
Beats:	1	2	3	4	1	2	3	4	1	2	3	4	1	2	3	4
LH:		G		G	A	B		G		G		G	A	B		

A Song for Both Hands: Twinkle, Twinkle, Little Star

> • If you see a blank space, don't play for that beat or beats.
> • Remember to place both of your thumbs on Middle C.

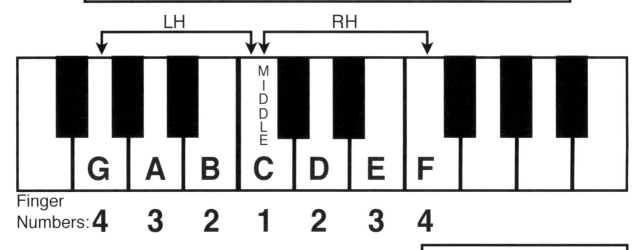

> • Try to count the beats aloud, while you play.

Twinkle, Twinkle

RH:		D	D		E	E	D		C	C							
4/4 Beats:	1	2	3	4	1	2	3	4	1	2	3	4	1	2	3	4	
LH:	G	G									B	B	A	A	G		

RH:	D	D	C	C						D	D	C	C				
Beats:	1	2	3	4	1	2	3	4	1	2	3	4	1	2	3	4	
LH:						B	B	A						B	B	A	

RH:		D	D		E	E	D		C	C							
Beats:	1	2	3	4	1	2	3	4	1	2	3	4	1	2	3	4	
LH:	G	G									B	B	A	A	G		

A Song for Both Hands:
The Ballgame

Let's add one more note for each hand: "F" in the Left Hand and "G" in the right hand. Both of these notes ("F" in LH and "G" in RH) will be played with the fifth finger (Pinky). Remember, the numbers in these songs are for the <u>beats</u>, not for the fingers.

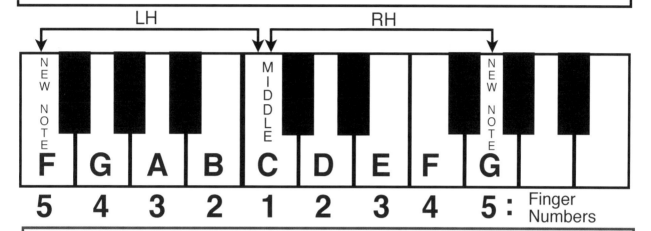

• Both Thumbs (RH and LH) share Middle C for this song.

• If there is a blank space, don't play for that beat or beats. In music,
• these silent beats are called "rests".

• We will learn more about rests later in this book.

The Ballgame

3/4

RH:			**F**	**D**	**C**		**C**					
Beats:	**1**	**2**	**3**	**1**	**2**	**3**	**1**	**2**	**3**	**1**	**2**	**3**
LH:	**F**					**A**				**G**		

RH:			**F**	**D**	**C**		**C**					
Beats:	**1**	**2**	**3**	**1**	**2**	**3**	**1**	**2**	**3**	**1**	**2**	**3**
LH:	**F**					**A**				**C**		

19

Music Theory: What are Intervals?

- In music, the distance between any 2 notes is called an "Interval".
- Intervals can be played at the same time, for example, if you press down two piano keys or they can be played one after the other, for example, if you play the note "C" and then the note "D".
- On the piano, the easiest way to understand intervals is to look at the keyboard. Play Middle C with your Left-Hand Index Finger, then play D with your Right-Hand Index finger. This interval is called a 2nd.
- Next, play Middle C with your Left-Hand Index Finger, then play E with your Right-Hand Index finger. This interval is called a 3rd.
- Follow these steps in the 2 diagrams below. Use the Left-Hand Index Finger when you see LH and use the Right-Hand Index Finger when you see RH.

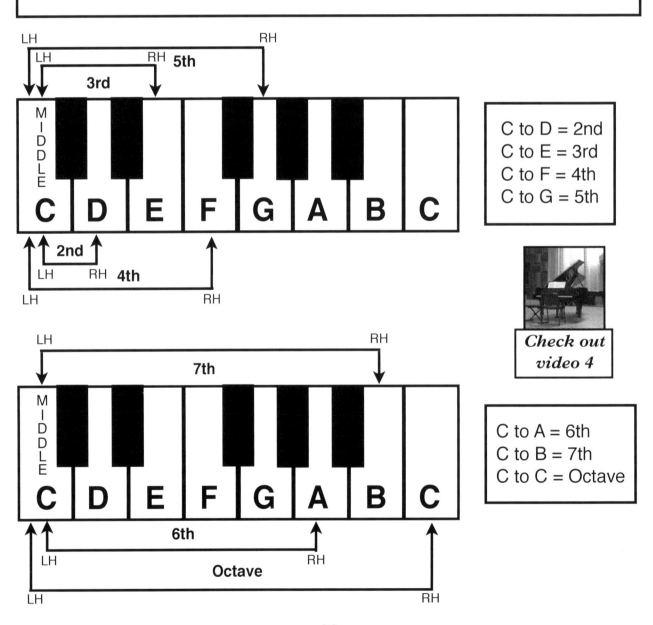

C to D = 2nd
C to E = 3rd
C to F = 4th
C to G = 5th

Check out video 4

C to A = 6th
C to B = 7th
C to C = Octave

Song for Both Hands: Fanfare

> • In these next songs, we will be playing notes with the Right Hand and Left Hand at the same time.
>
> • When one letter is on top of another letter, play both at the same time. *Have Fun!*

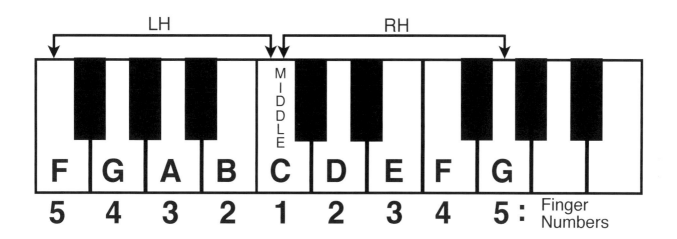

Fanfare

RH:	G G G G	E E E E	F F F F	E E E E
4/4 Beats:	1 2 3 4	1 2 3 4	1 2 3 4	1 2 3 4
LH:	C C C C	C C C C	C C C C	C C C C

RH:	G G G G	E E E E	F F F F	C
Beats:	1 2 3 4	1 2 3 4	1 2 3 4	1 2 3 4
LH:	C C C C	C C C C	C C C C	G

Songs for Both Hands: Love Somebody & Snow

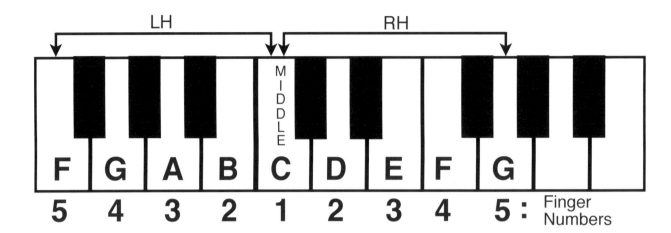

Love Somebody

RH: C E G G | D E F | C E G G | F E D |
Beats: 1 2 3 4 | 1 2 3 4 | 1 2 3 4 | 1 2 3 4 |
LH: G | G | G | A |

RH: C E G G | D E F | E E D D | C C C |
Beats: 1 2 3 4 | 1 2 3 4 | 1 2 3 4 | 1 2 3 4 |
LH: G | G | G | G |

Snow

RH: E | E | D D D D | C C C C |
Beats: 1 2 3 4 | 1 2 3 4 | 1 2 3 4 | 1 2 3 4 |
LH: A B C B | A B C B | B B B B | A A A A |

Songs for Both Hands:
Ode to Joy & Summer Evening

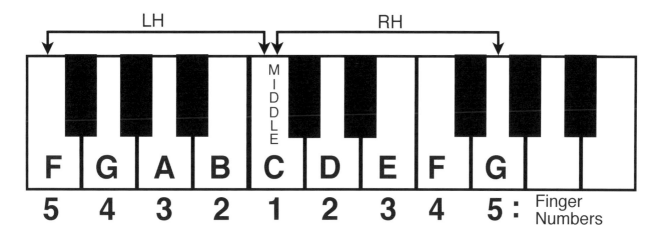

5 4 3 2 1 2 3 4 5 : Finger Numbers

Ode to Joy

Try this more advanced version of Beethoven's *Ode to Joy.*

$\frac{4}{4}$ Beats:

E E F G	G F E D	C C D E	E D D
1 2 3 4	1 2 3 4	1 2 3 4	1 2 3 4
G	C	A	G

E E F G	G F E D	C C D E	D C C
1 2 3 4	1 2 3 4	1 2 3 4	1 2 3 4
G	C	A	G

Summer Evening

$\frac{4}{4}$ Beats:

RH: G E	F D	E C	C C
1 2 3 4	1 2 3 4	1 2 3 4	1 2 3 4
LH: C C	B B	A A	G B

23

Upbeats & When the Saints Go Marching In

- In music, there are many songs and pieces that use Upbeats.
- An Upbeat (or Upbeats) is a note or group of notes that occur before the first full measure of a song or piece of music.
- Upbeats act as very short introductory phrases that emphasize an important note or word at the beginning of a song. For example, in *When the Saints Go Marching In,* the words "Oh when the" are the upbeat. They lead into and accentuate the word "saints".

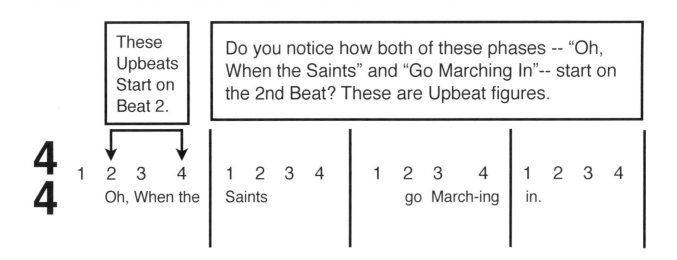

These Upbeats Start on Beat 2.

Do you notice how both of these phases -- "Oh, When the Saints" and "Go Marching In"-- start on the 2nd Beat? These are Upbeat figures.

$\frac{4}{4}$

| 1 | 2 | 3 | 4 | 1 | 2 | 3 | 4 | 1 | 2 | 3 | 4 | 1 | 2 | 3 | 4 |
Oh, When the | Saints | go March-ing | in.

When the Saints Go Marching In

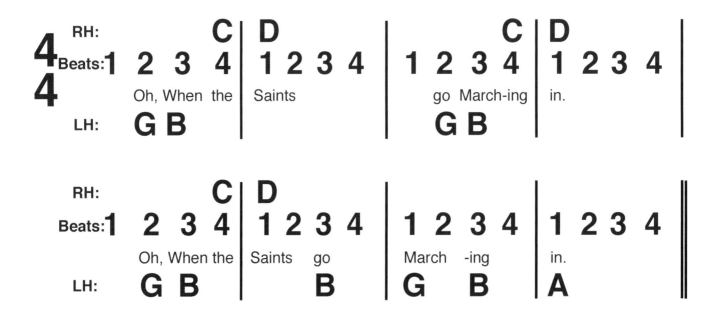

Whole Notes, Half Notes
& Quarter Notes

- Let's take a look at some basic rhythms.
- Quarter Notes are notes that get 1 Beat (or Count).
- Half Notes are notes that get 2 Beats (or Counts).
- Whole Notes are notes that get 4 Beats (or Counts).
- In the next 3 examples, try counting on each beat of the 4/4 measures aloud, for example: 1,2,3,4.
- Clap on the quarter, half, and whole notes.

Check out video 5

♩ = 1 Beat   ♩ = 2 Beats   o = 4 Beats

Example 1:
Try Clapping on each "X", while counting the beats.

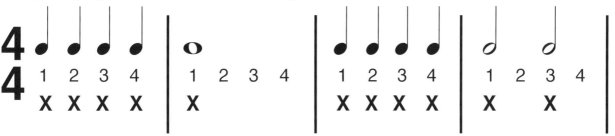

Example 2:
Try Clapping on each "X", while counting the beats.

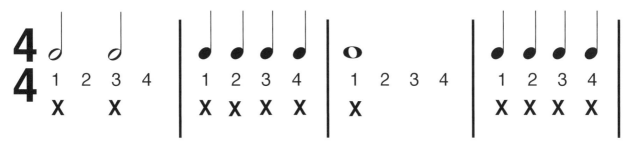

Example 3:
Try Clapping on each "X", while counting the beats.

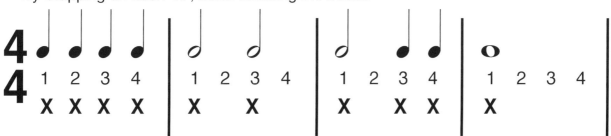

Songs with Half Notes
& Quarter Notes

- Try these songs that use Half Notes (2 beats or counts) and quarter notes (1 beat or count).

- All of the songs on this page are for the Right Hand (RH).

- Try to count aloud (1,2,3,4) for each measure.

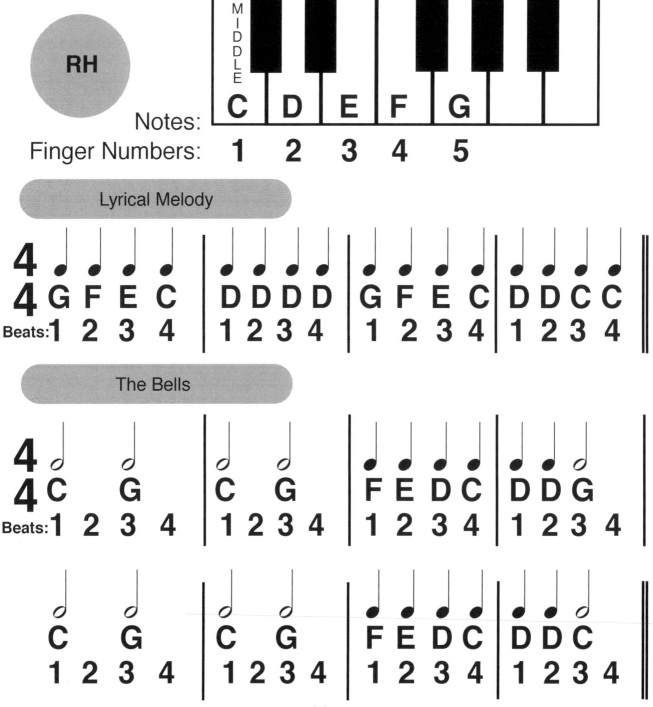

Five-Note Songs with Half Notes & Quarter Notes

- Try these songs that use Half Notes (2 beats or counts) and Quarter Notes (1 beat or count).
- All of the songs on this page are for the Right Hand (RH).
- Try to count aloud (1,2,3,4) for each measure.

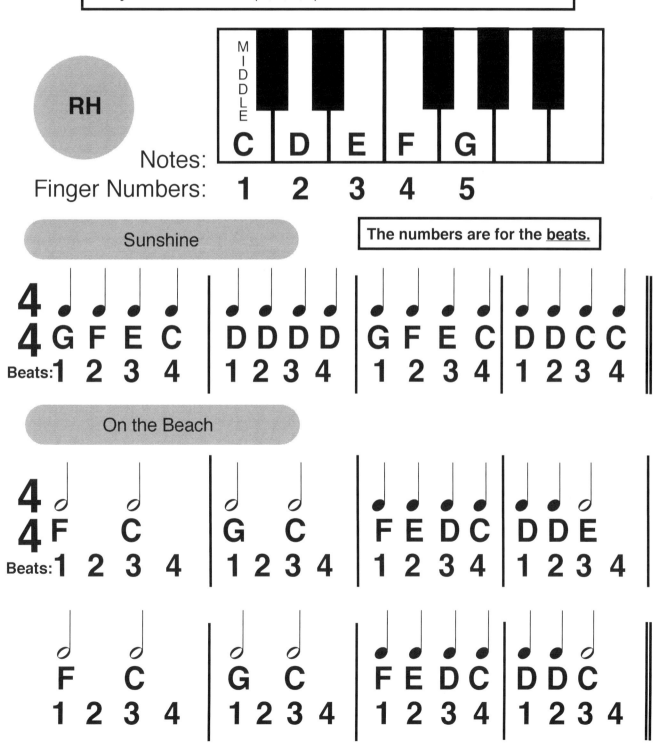

Notes:

Finger Numbers: **1 2 3 4 5**

Sunshine

The numbers are for the beats.

$\frac{4}{4}$ G F E C | D D D D | G F E C | D D C C ‖
Beats: 1 2 3 4 | 1 2 3 4 | 1 2 3 4 | 1 2 3 4

On the Beach

$\frac{4}{4}$ F C | G C | F E D C | D D E
Beats: 1 2 3 4 | 1 2 3 4 | 1 2 3 4 | 1 2 3 4

F C | G C | F E D C | D D C ‖
1 2 3 4 | 1 2 3 4 | 1 2 3 4 | 1 2 3 4

Five-Note Songs with Whole, Half & Quarter Notes

• Try these songs that use Quarter Notes (1 beat), Half
  Notes (2 beats) and Whole Notes (4 beats).
• All of the songs on this page are for the Right Hand (RH).
• Try to count aloud (1,2,3,4) for each measure.

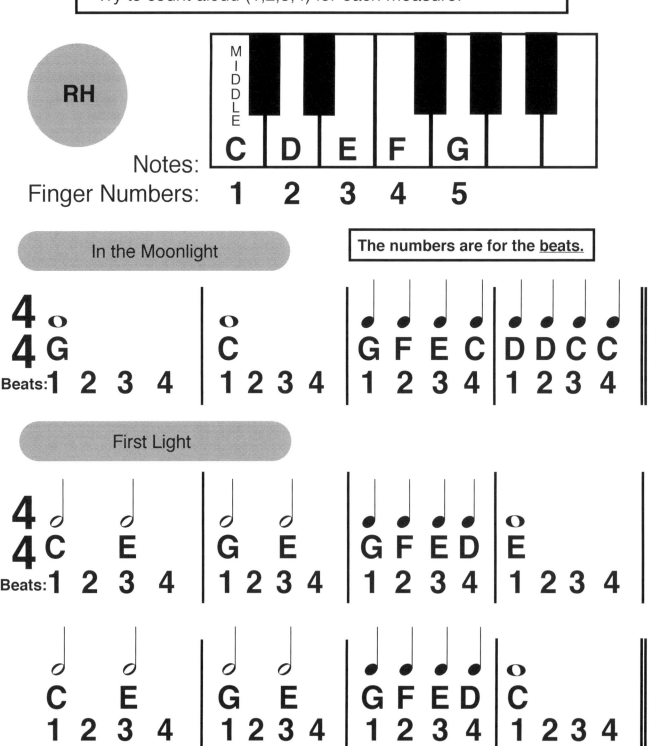

Five-Note Songs with Half Notes & Quarter Notes

- Try these songs that use Half Notes (2 beats or counts) and quarter notes (1 beat or count).
- All of the songs on this page are for the Left Hand (LH).
- Try to count aloud (1,2,3,4) for each measure.

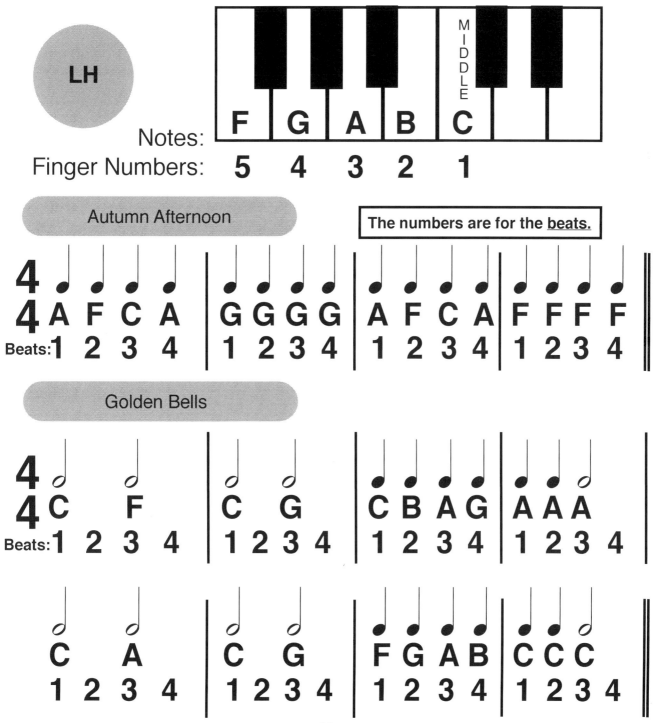

LH

Notes: F G A B C
Finger Numbers: 5 4 3 2 1

Autumn Afternoon

The numbers are for the <u>beats.</u>

4/4
A F C A | G G G G | A F C A | F F F F ||
Beats: 1 2 3 4 | 1 2 3 4 | 1 2 3 4 | 1 2 3 4

Golden Bells

4/4
C   F | C   G | C B A G | A A A |
Beats: 1 2 3 4 | 1 2 3 4 | 1 2 3 4 | 1 2 3 4

C   A | C   G | F G A B | C C C ||
1 2 3 4 | 1 2 3 4 | 1 2 3 4 | 1 2 3 4

29

Five-Note Songs with Half, Whole, & Quarter Notes Whole Notes for the Left Hand

- Try these songs that use Quarter Notes (1 beat), Half Notes (2 beats) and Whole Notes (4 beats or counts).
- All of the songs on this page are for the Left Hand (LH).
- Try to count aloud (1,2,3,4) for each measure.

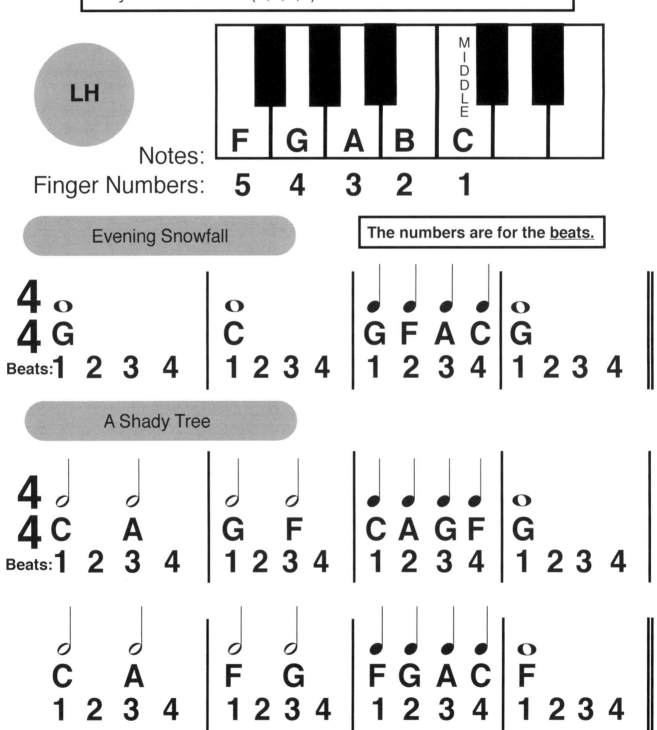

LH

Notes: F G A B C (MIDDLE)

Finger Numbers: 5 4 3 2 1

Evening Snowfall

The numbers are for the **beats.**

4/4 G | C | G F A C G
Beats: 1 2 3 4 | 1 2 3 4 | 1 2 3 4 | 1 2 3 4

A Shady Tree

4/4 C A | G F | C A G F G
Beats: 1 2 3 4 | 1 2 3 4 | 1 2 3 4 | 1 2 3 4

C A | F G | F G A C F
1 2 3 4 | 1 2 3 4 | 1 2 3 4 | 1 2 3 4

Treble Clef Notes: Middle C, D & E

- The Treble Clef mainly is used for notes above Middle C.
- About 90% of the time, it is used for the Right Hand.
  (There are a few occasions in songs or pieces when it is used for the Left Hand.)
- The Treble Clef is made up of Lines and Spaces that correspond to keys on the piano. Each Line or Space is linked to <u>one</u> (and only one) key on the piano.
- We will learn more about the lines and spaces of the Treble Clef in the following lessons.

Check out video 6

Middle C

Middle C is under the Treble Clef. There is a line through the middle of the note.

This is the TrebleClef Symbol:

Note:

Finger Number: **1**

RH

D

D is under the Treble Clef, as well. It hangs under the lowest line of the Treble Clef.

Note:

Finger Number: **2**

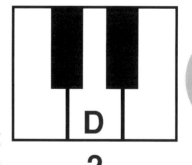

RH

E

E is on the first line of the Treble Clef.

Note:

Finger Number: **3**

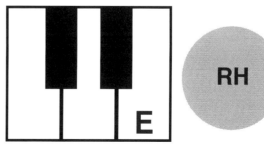

RH

Treble Clef Exercises: Middle C, D, and E (RH)

> • Let's play 4 songs with notes of the Treble Clef: C, D, and E.
>
> • Remember to find Middle C with the Thumb of your right hand.

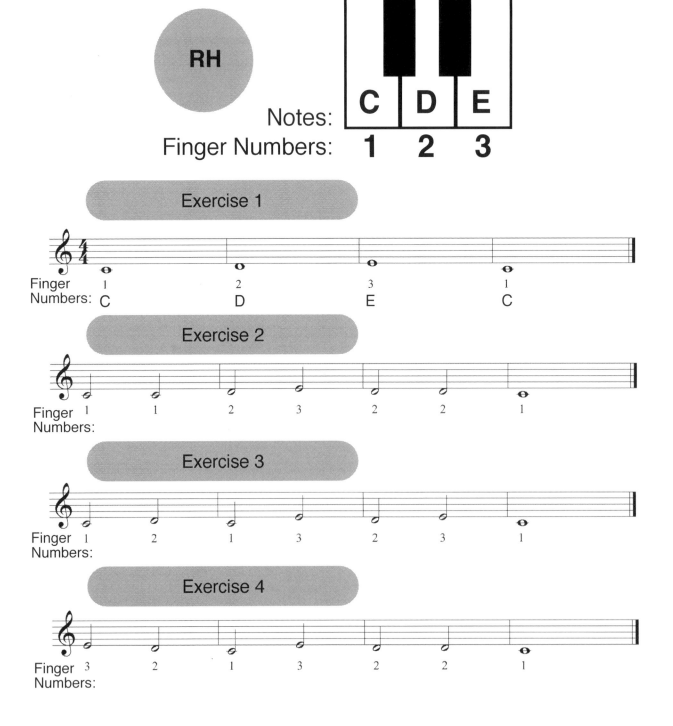

RH

Notes: C D E
Finger Numbers: **1** **2** **3**

Exercise 1

Finger Numbers: 1 C 2 D 3 E 1 C

Exercise 2

Finger Numbers: 1 1 2 3 2 2 1

Exercise 3

Finger Numbers: 1 2 1 3 2 3 1

Exercise 4

Finger Numbers: 3 2 1 3 2 2 1

More Treble Clef Exercises: Middle C, D, E, & F (RH)

- Let's add the note F, which is on the 1st space of the Treble Clef.
- Remember to find Middle C with the Thumb of your right hand (RH).

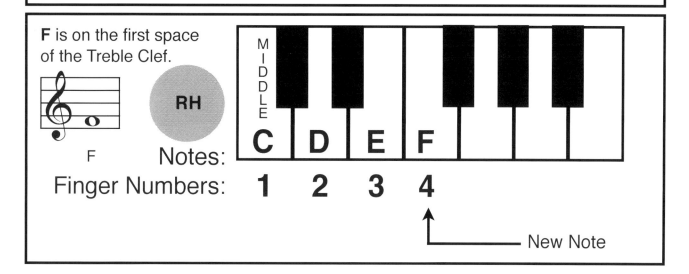

F is on the first space of the Treble Clef.

F

RH

Notes: C D E F

Finger Numbers: 1 2 3 4

New Note

Exercise 1

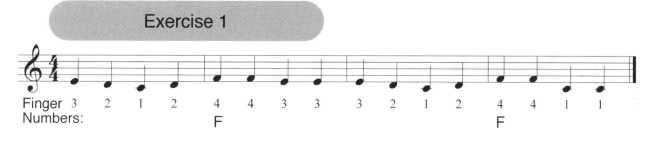

Finger Numbers: 3 2 1 2 4 4 3 3 3 2 1 2 4 4 1 1
F   F

Exercise 2

Finger Numbers: 1 3 2 4 3 2 1 2 2 1
F

Exercise 3

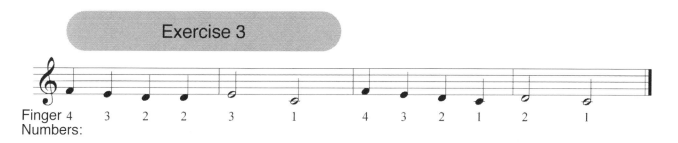

Finger Numbers: 4 3 2 2 3 1 4 3 2 1 2 1

Overview: The Treble Clef Lines

- Each line of the Treble Clef stands for a specific note and key on the piano.
- The lines have numbers that go from 1 to 5. Line 1 is the lowest line. Line 5 is the top line (or highest line) on the Treble Clef.
- To help you remember the note names of each line, memorize the saying below. In the saying ("Every Good Bird Does Fly"). "Every" stands for "E", "Good" stands for "G", "Bird" stands for "B", "Does" stands for "D", and "Fly" stands for "F".
- The "E" of "Every" stands for the "E" piano key 2 notes above Middle C. See the charts below to better understand these notes.

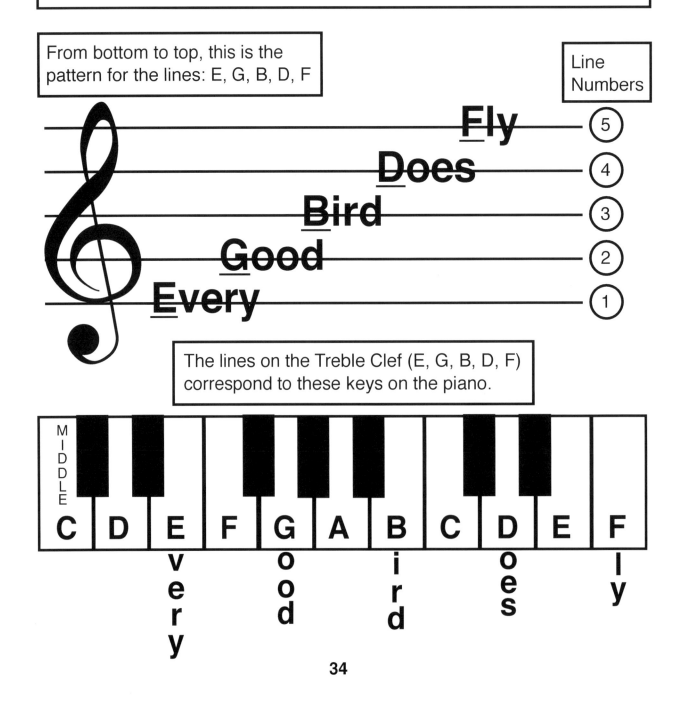

From bottom to top, this is the pattern for the lines: E, G, B, D, F

Line Numbers

Fly — 5
Does — 4
Bird — 3
Good — 2
Every — 1

The lines on the Treble Clef (E, G, B, D, F) correspond to these keys on the piano.

Overview: The Treble Clef Spaces

- Each space of the Treble Clef stands for a specific note and key on the piano keyboard.
- The spaces have numbers that go from 1 to 4. Space 1 is the lowest space. Space 4 is the top space (or highest space) on the Treble Clef.
- To help you learn the note names of each space, remember that the spaces of the Treble Clef form the word "Face" spelled upside down (from bottom space to top.)
- The "F" of "Face" stands for the "F" piano key 4 notes above Middle C.
- See the charts below to better understand the other notes.
- Video Lesson 6 goes over this material in addition detail.

From bottom to top, this is the pattern for the Spaces: F, A, C, E

Space Numbers

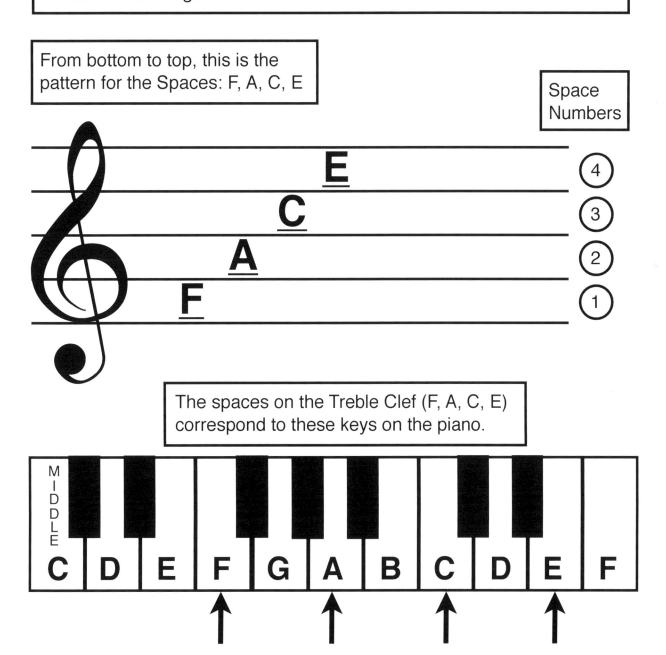

The spaces on the Treble Clef (F, A, C, E) correspond to these keys on the piano.

Kum-Bah-Yah
& New Notes: G & A

- Let's add 2 new notes G and A, which are on the 2nd line and space of the Treble Clef. To play the note A, move your fifth finger one key higher.
- Remember to find Middle C with the Thumb of your right hand (RH).

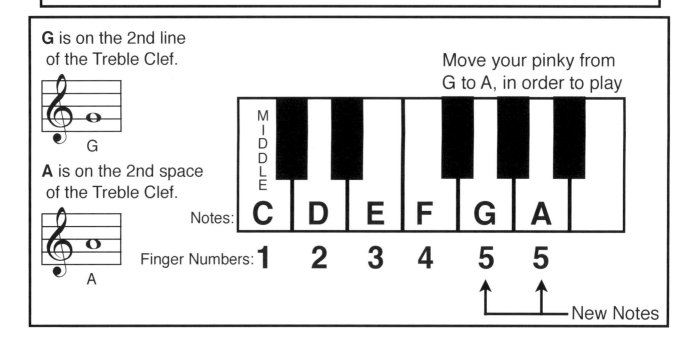

G is on the 2nd line of the Treble Clef.

A is on the 2nd space of the Treble Clef.

Move your pinky from G to A, in order to play

Notes: C D E F G A

Finger Numbers: 1 2 3 4 5 5

New Notes

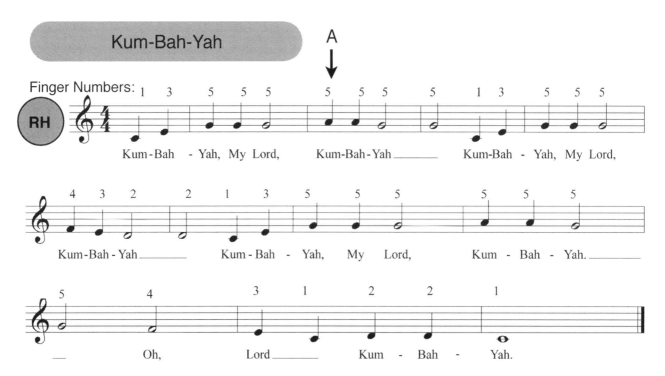

Kum-Bah-Yah

A

Finger Numbers:

RH

1 3 5 5 5 5 5 5 5 1 3 5 5 5

Kum-Bah - Yah, My Lord, Kum-Bah-Yah_____ Kum-Bah - Yah, My Lord,

4 3 2 2 1 3 5 5 5 5 5 5

Kum-Bah - Yah_____ Kum - Bah - Yah, My Lord, Kum - Bah - Yah._____

5 4 3 1 2 2 1

___ Oh, Lord_____ Kum - Bah - Yah.

36

Bass Clef Notes: Middle C, B & A

- The Bass Clef mainly is used for notes below Middle C.
- About 90% of the time, it is used for the Left Hand.
  (There are a few occasions in songs and pieces of music when the Bass Clef is used for the Right Hand.)
- The word "Bass" is pronounced like the word "Base" (as in "Baseball").
- The Bass Clef is made up of Lines and Spaces that correspond to keys on the piano. Each Line or Space is linked to <u>one</u> (and only one) key on the piano keyboard.
- We will learn more about the lines and spaces of the Bass Clef in the following lessons.

Check out video 7

Middle C

This is the Bass Clef Symbol: 𝄢

Middle C is above the Bass Clef. There is a line through the middle of the note.

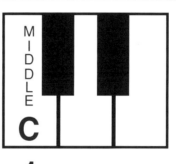

Note:

Finger Number: **1**

B

B is on the Bass Clef. It sits on top of the highest line of the Bass Clef.

Note:

Finger Number: **2**

A

A is on the fifth line of the Bass Clef.

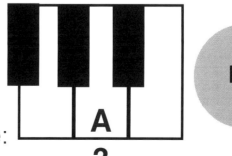

Note:

Finger Number: **3**

The Bass Clef Exercises: A, B and Middle C

- Let's play these four exercises with notes of the Bass Clef: A, B, and C.

- Remember to find Middle C with the Thumb of your left hand (LH).

LH

MIDDLE

Notes: A B C

Finger Numbers: 3 2 1

Try saying the notes aloud as you play each song.

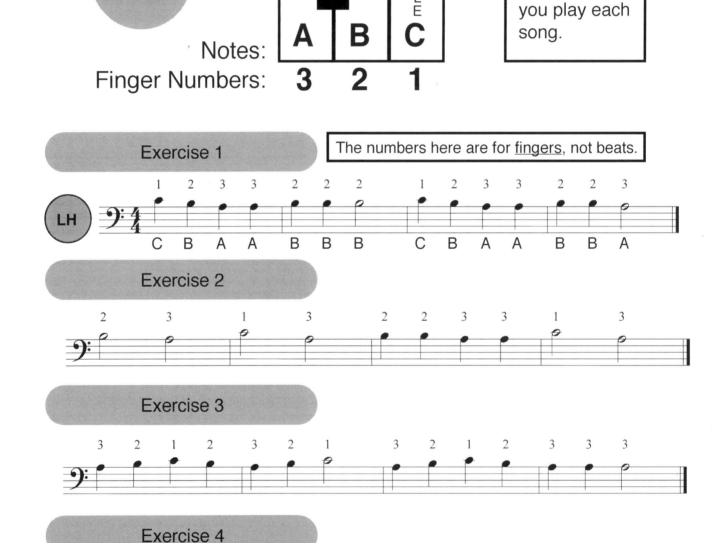

Exercise 1

The numbers here are for <u>fingers</u>, not beats.

LH

1 2 3 3 2 2 2   1 2 3 3 2 2 3

C B A A B B B   C B A A B B A

Exercise 2

2   3   1   3   2 2 3 3 1   3

Exercise 3

3 2 1 2 3 2 1   3 2 1 2 3 3 3

Exercise 4

1 3 1 3 2 2 1   1 3 2 3 1 1 3

More Bass Clef Exercises:
G, A, B and Middle C

- Let's add the note G, which is on the 4th space of the Bass Clef.

- Remember to find Middle C with the Thumb of your left hand (LH).

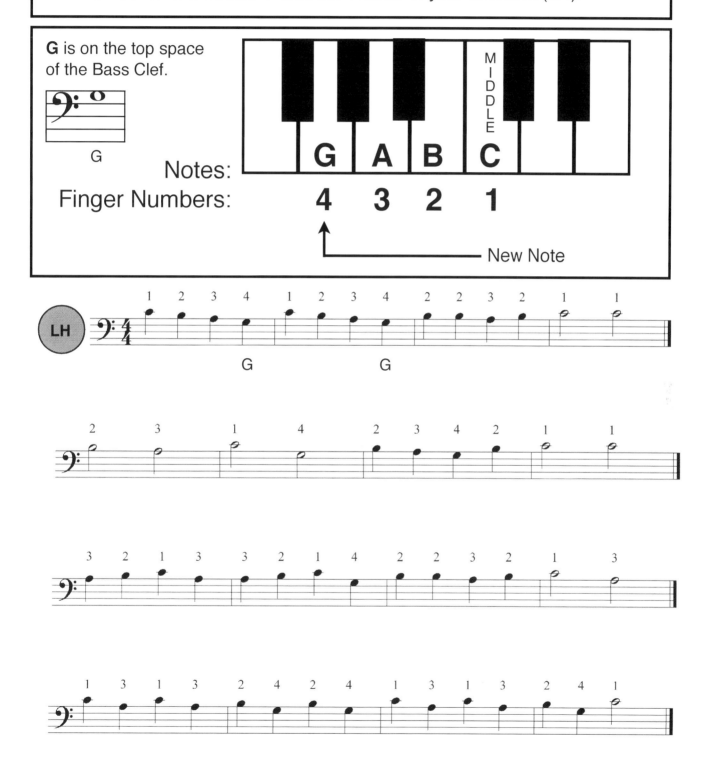

G is on the top space of the Bass Clef.

G

Notes:
Finger Numbers:

G A B C

4 3 2 1

New Note

Overview: The Bass Clef Lines

- Each line of the Bass Clef stands for a specific note and key on the piano.
- The lines have numbers that go from 1 to 5. Line 1 is the lowest line. Line 5 is the top line (or highest line) on the Bass Clef.
- To help you remember the note names of each line, memorize the saying below. In the saying ("Good Baked Desserts For All"). "Good" stands for "G", "Baked" stands for "B", "Desserts" stands for "D", "For" stands for "F", and "All" stands for "A".
- The "A" of "All" stands for the "A" piano key 2 notes below Middle C. See the charts below to better understand these notes.

From bottom to top, this is the pattern for the lines: G, B, D, F, A

Line Numbers

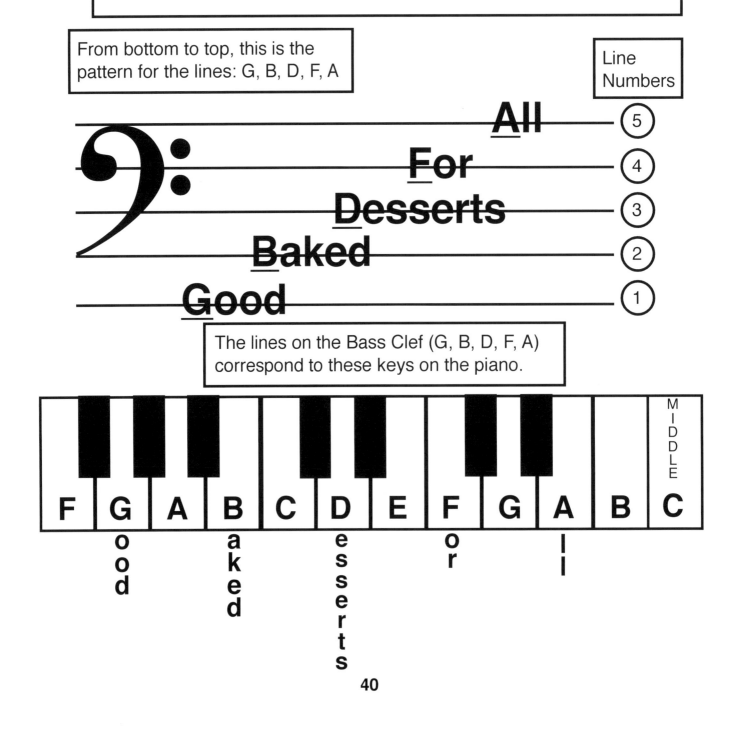

The lines on the Bass Clef (G, B, D, F, A) correspond to these keys on the piano.

Overview: The Bass Clef Spaces

- Each space of the Bass Clef stands for a specific note and key on the piano.
- The spaces have numbers that go from 1 to 4. Space 1 is the lowest space. Space 4 is the top space (or highest space) on the Bass Clef.
- To help you learn the note names of each space, remember that the spaces of the Bass Clef form the phrase "All cows eat grass".
- The word "All" stands for the key and note "A"; the word "Cows" stands for "C"; the word "Eat" stands for "E"; the word "Grass" stands for "G".
- See the charts below to better understand the other notes.

Space Numbers

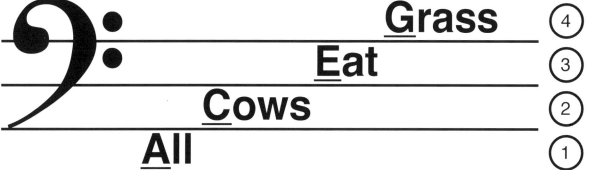

The spaces on the Bass Clef (A, C, E, G) correspond to these keys on the piano.

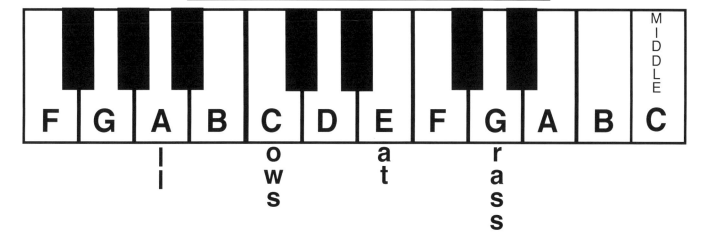

Bass Clef Exercise:
F, G, A, B, and Middle C

- Let's add the note F, which is on the 4th line of the Bass Clef.

- Remember to find Middle C with the Thumb of your left hand (LH).

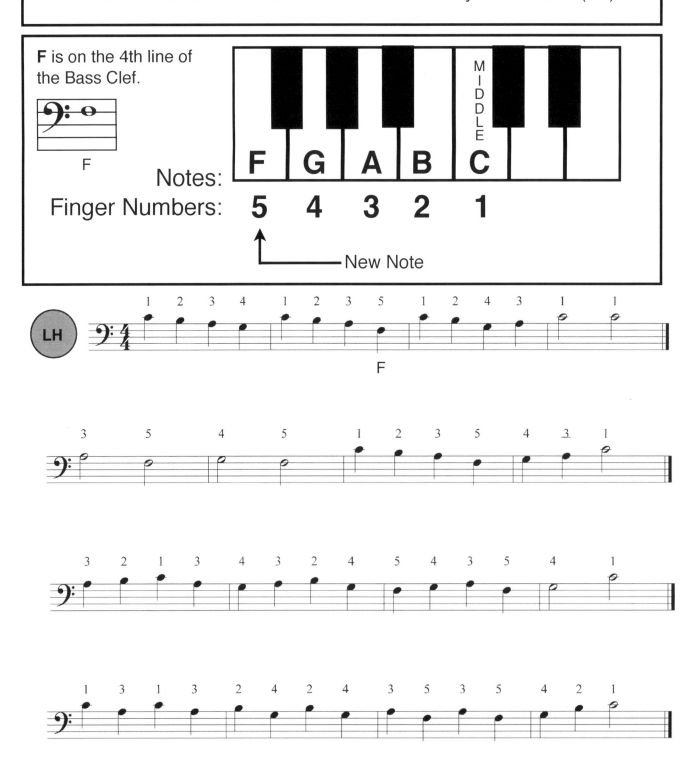

Bass Clef Exercises:
F, G, A, B, and Middle C

• Let's add the note F, which is on the 4th line of the Bass Clef.

• Remember to find Middle C with the Thumb of your left hand (LH).

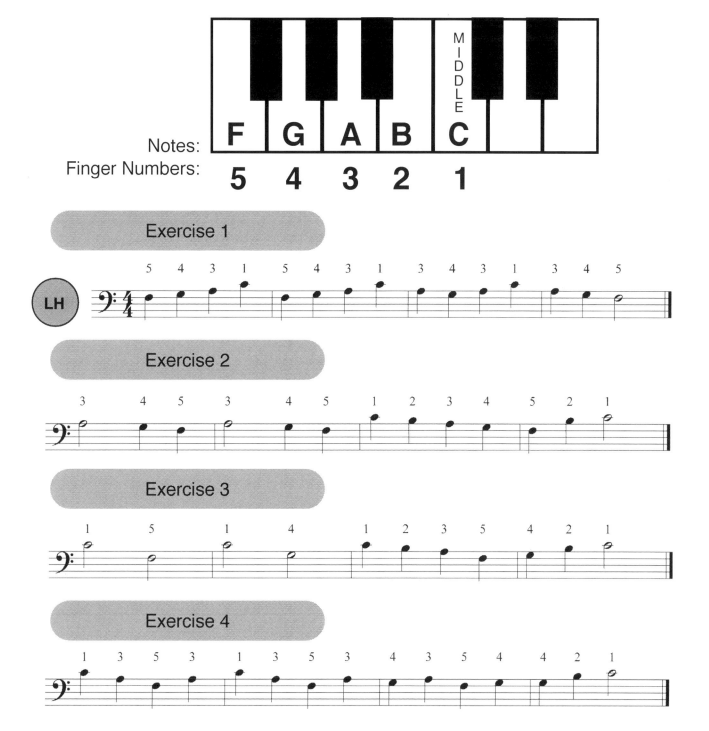

Studies for the Left Hand: Grieg's Hall of the Mountain King & Pachelbel's Canon

These next two pieces are studies for the left hand. To help you out, the letter names are written inside of the notes.

For Grieg's *Hall of the Mountain King*, start with the fifth finger (pinky) of your left hand on the key of D, which is seven keys below middle C. The notes for hand position one are D, E, F, G and A. In measure six of the piece, you will shift your hand position and play the A with the third finger (middle finger) of your left hand. The notes for hand position two are F, A, middle C and D.

For Pachelbel's *Canon*, there are four easy left-hand positions. Each hand position uses only three fingers: thumb, index, and middle finger. You will start on middle C for hand position one. For hand position two, you will move your thumb to G (the top space of the bass clef). In hand position three, you will move your thumb to E (just two notes above middle C). Place your thumb on B (just below middle C) for hand position number four. For the last note of the piece (C), just move your thumb one key higher than B (to middle C).

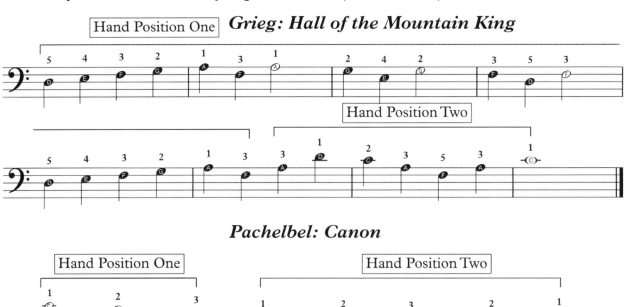

Grieg: Hall of the Mountain King

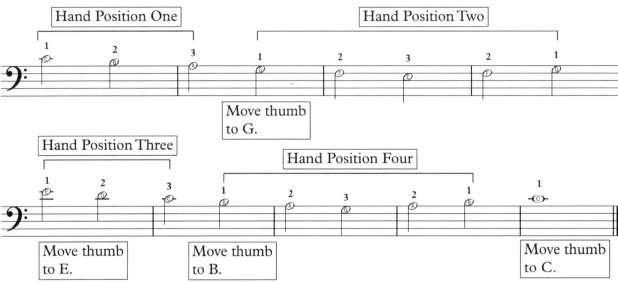

Pachelbel: Canon

44

Overview: The Grand Staff

- The Grand Staff is formed by combining the Treble and Bass Clefs.
- All of the rules that we have learned so far about both clefs are still true for the Grand Staff. Using the Grand Staff makes it easier to read music written for both hands.
- Study the chart below to understand how the Staff works.

Check out video 8

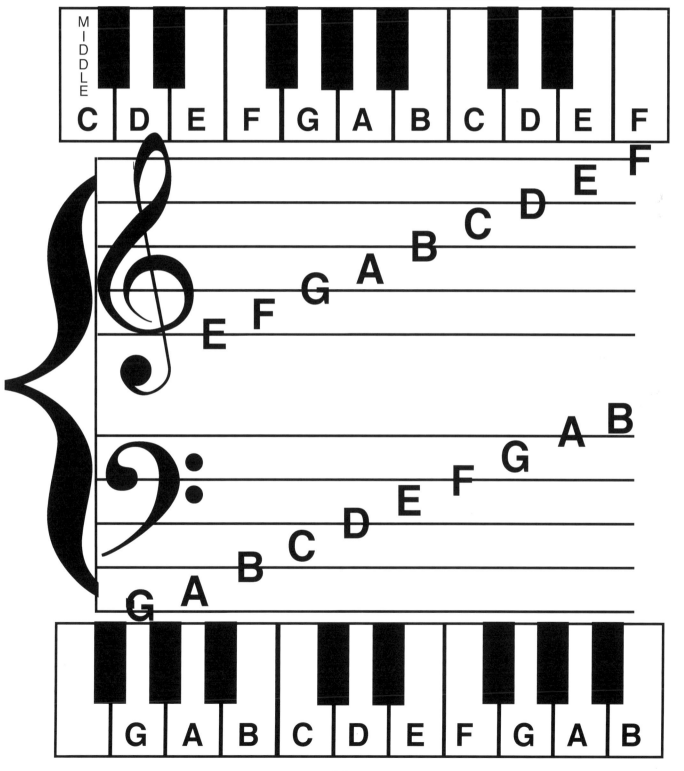

Naming the Notes on the Grand Staff

For this lesson, let's try naming the notes on the grand staff below. Remember to use your note-name sayings from earlier in the book. You may also refer back to the grand staff on the previous page. Try naming the notes for one measure, then go back and repeat naming the notes for that measure three times. Once you feel confident about the note names, go on to the next measure. After you have finished naming the notes on the entire page, go back to the beginning of the lesson and slowly play each note on the piano. You might also say the note aloud as you play it. This will begin to reinforce your understanding of the notes on the page and the keys on the piano keyboard.

Section 2
Famous Songs &
Pieces of Music

Section 2: Famous Songs & Pieces of Music

Throughout Section 2, we will go over strategies that will make learning each piece of music easier for you. As we get started with this section, I would like to mention one approach that will greatly aid in your learning these pieces:

Try this: Focus on learning only one or two measures at a time, starting with the right hand, then the left hand, and, finally, when you have mastered playing the music for each hand separately, play both hands together. Then, repeat this process for learning the next measure or two measures of the piece. This approach will greatly speed up your learning. It will also make your playing of the pieces much more secure. Please focus on this approach in your practice sessions, rather than only playing the song or piece from beginning to end.

Here are some of the concepts and techniques that you will learn, along with the pieces, in this section of the book:

- dynamics
- crescendo and diminuendo markings
- dotted eighth notes
- subdividing
- coordinating both hands
- counting beats
- reading in both clefs
- slurs: phase markers
- left-hand accompaniment styles
- upbeats
- thumb-under technique
- ties

Simple Gifts

For *Simple Gifts,* your right-hand thumb will be on Middle C. Your left-hand thumb should be placed on the B, directly to the left of Middle C. (See chart below.)

To make the music easier to read, the note names are written inside of the notes and the finger numbers are indicated above the notes.

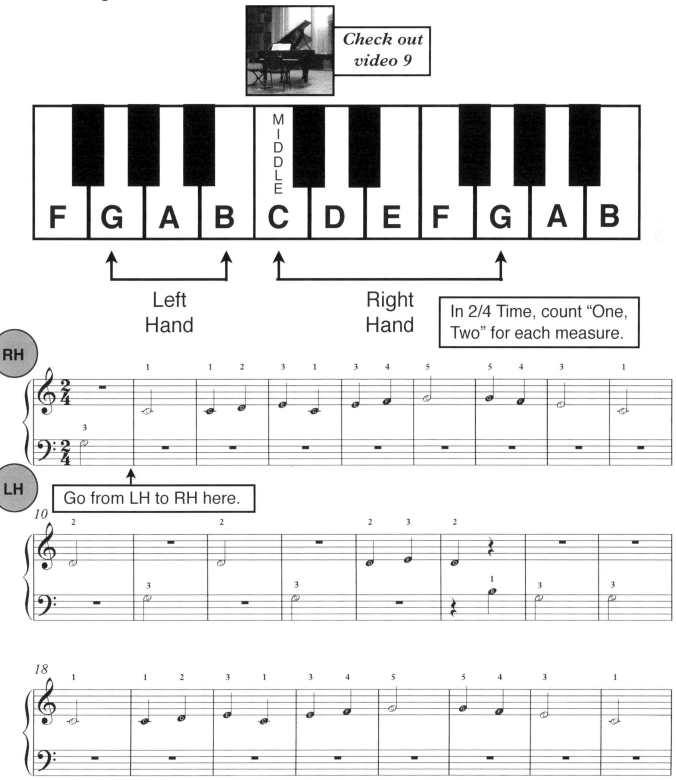

Check out video 9

Left Hand

Right Hand

In 2/4 Time, count "One, Two" for each measure.

Go from LH to RH here.

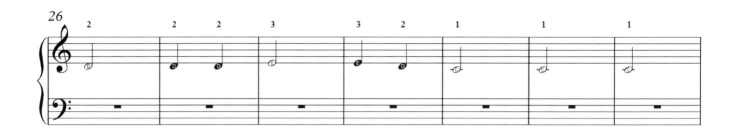

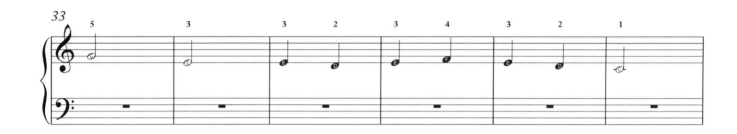

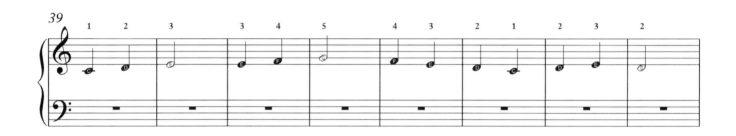

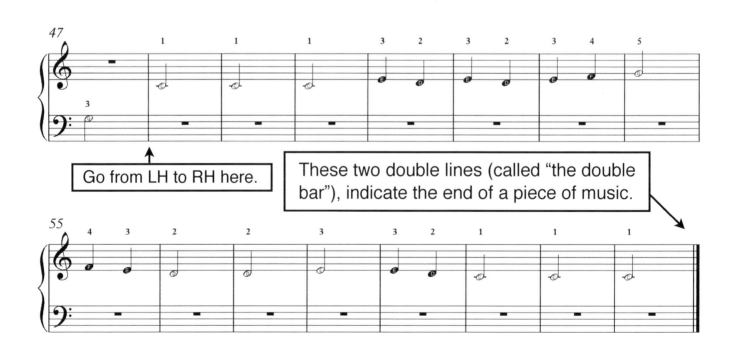

Go from LH to RH here.

These two double lines (called "the double bar"), indicate the end of a piece of music.

Amazing Grace

- *Amazing Grace* is in 3/4 Time. Remember to count "One, Two, Three" for each measure.
- The melody goes between the left and right hands many times.
- Please hold the dotted half note for three beats (or counts). See the example below:

♩. = 3 Beats

Check out video 10

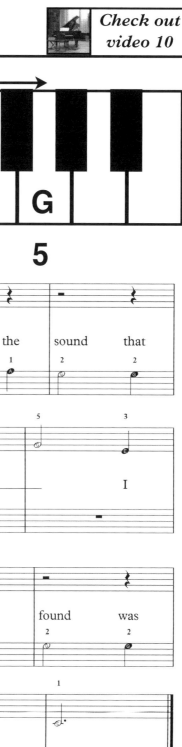

Finger Numbers: **2   1   1   2   3   4   5**

A - ma - zing Grace how sweet the sound that

saved a wretch like me. _____ I

once was lost, but now I'm found was

blind, but now I see.

Jingle Bells

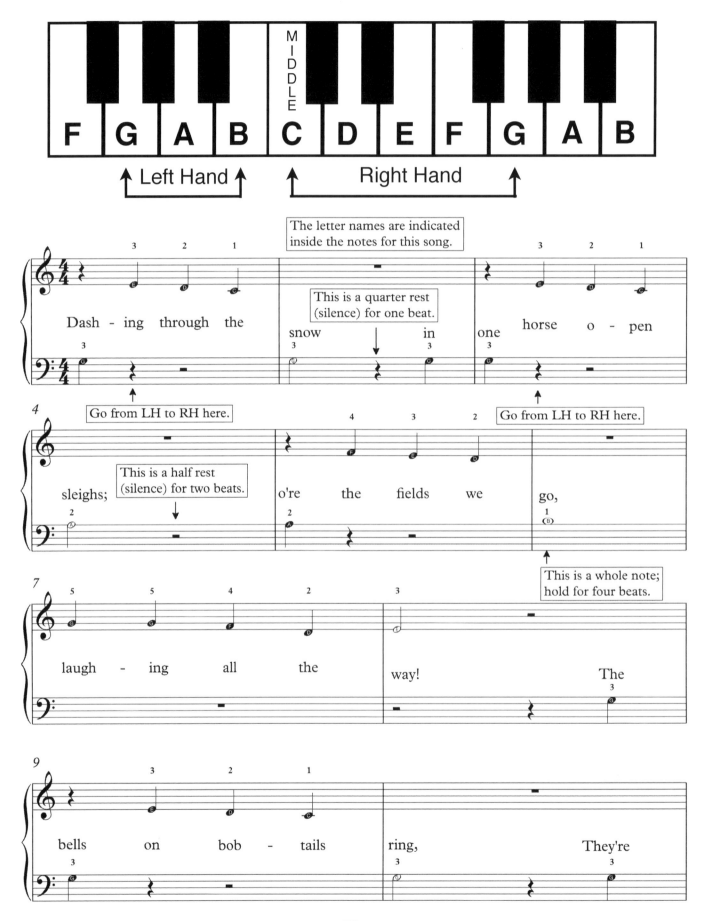

Michael, Row the Boat Ashore

- *Michael, Row the Boat Ashore* is in 4/4 Time. Remember to count "One, Two, Three, Four" for each measure.
- Both right-hand and left-hand thumbs share Middle C.
- This song also goes back and forth between the hands. Take a glance at the music and look for patterns of hand switching before you start playing the music.
- Lastly, we have left out the letter names from inside the notes for this song. Refer back to the Grand Staff, if you have questions.

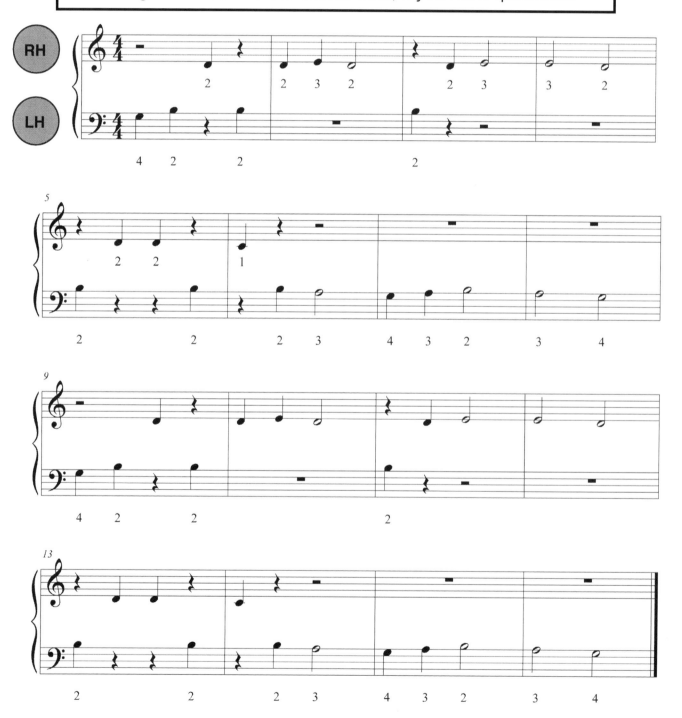

In May

> • Slurs (or Phrase Markers) are curved lines that go over or under two or more different notes in piano music.
> • They indicate two things: to play a passage or phrase with a smooth sound ("legato", which means smooth or connected notes played) and slurs (or phrase markers) also indicate where a musical phrase (the musical equivalent to a sentence) starts and ends.
> • For *In May*, both the right-hand and left-hand thumbs will share Middle C. Before playing the piece, take a glance at the page and make a note of the places where the melody goes from the right hand to the left hand. Try to anticipate these shifts while you play the piece.

A Slur (or Phrase Marker)
looks like this: ⟶

Danny Boy

This is the main hand position for *Danny Boy*. The left-hand thumb will be on the E above Middle C and the right-hand thumb will be on F.

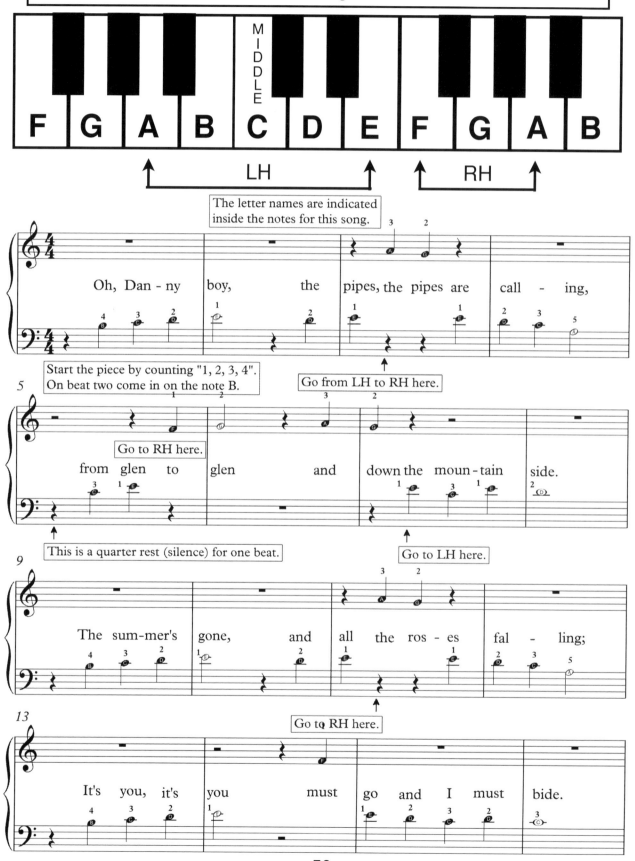

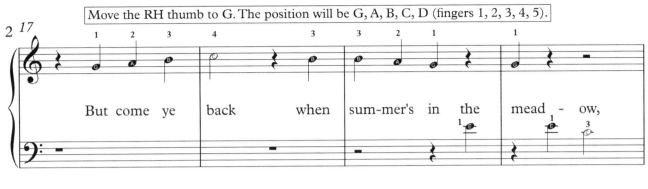

Move the RH thumb to G. The position will be G, A, B, C, D (fingers 1, 2, 3, 4, 5).

But come ye back when sum-mer's in the mead - ow,

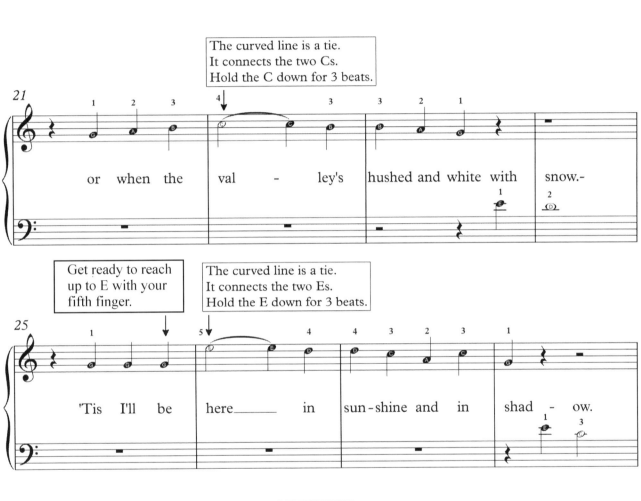

The curved line is a tie.
It connects the two Cs.
Hold the C down for 3 beats.

or when the val - ley's hushed and white with snow.-

Get ready to reach up to E with your fifth finger.

The curved line is a tie.
It connects the two Es.
Hold the E down for 3 beats.

'Tis I'll be here_____ in sun-shine and in shad - ow.

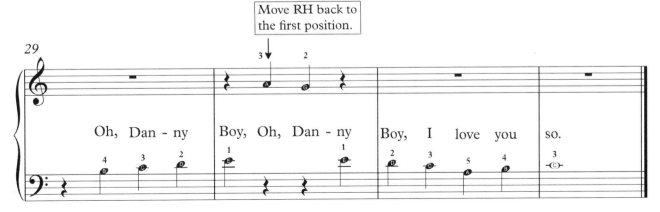

Move RH back to the first position.

Oh, Dan - ny Boy, Oh, Dan - ny Boy, I love you so.

Music Theory:

What are Sharps & Flats?

- On the piano, there are two types of keys: Black Keys and White Keys.
- The White Keys stand for natural notes, for example, C, D, E, F, G, A and B.
- The Black Keys (also called "accidentals") stand for Sharp or Flat Notes.
- Sharp Notes use this symbol: #
- Flat Notes use this symbol: ♭
- Here are some examples of Sharp Notes: F#, G#, A#, C#, D#
- Here are some examples of Flat Notes: Gb, Ab, Bb, Db, Eb

- On the piano keyboard, Sharp Keys are located directly to the right of their corresponding Natural Key (White Key). For example, F Sharp (F#) is the next key to the right from F (also called "F Natural"). C Sharp (C#) is the black key directly to the right of C (also called "C Natural").
- This pattern, of going to the next key directly to the right, holds true for all of the sharp notes going up and down the piano keyboard.
- Using the chart below, try locating the following sharp keys on the piano: C#, F#, D#, A#, G#.

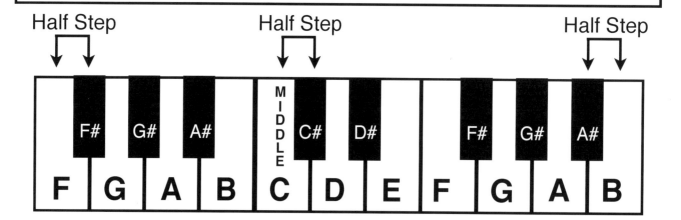

- The distance from a White Key to a Black Key, for example, F to F#, C to C#, or A# to B, is called a **Half Step** or Minor Second. **Remember this.** It is a bit of important information; we will be referring to it later in this book.

Music Theory
More on Flats and Sharps

- On the piano keyboard, Flat Keys are located directly to the left of their corresponding Natural Key (White Key). For example, G Flat (Gb) is the next black key to the left from G (also called "G Natural"). E Flat (Eb) is the black key directly to the left of E (also called "E Natural").
- This pattern, of going to the next key directly to the left, holds true for all of the flat notes going up and down the piano keyboard.
- Using the chart below, try locating the following flat keys on the piano: Ab, Db, Gb, Eb, Bb. **Remember: This pattern is the same for the entire keyboard.**

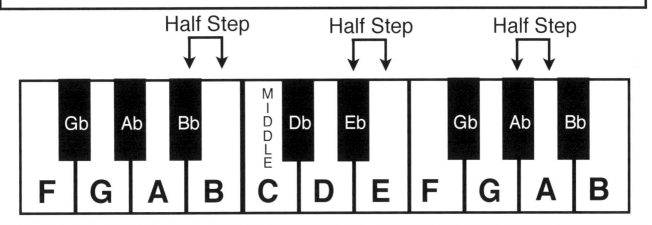

- The distance (up or down) from a White Key to a Black Key, for example, from B to Bb, Eb to E, or A to Ab, is called a Half Step or Minor Second. See Above.

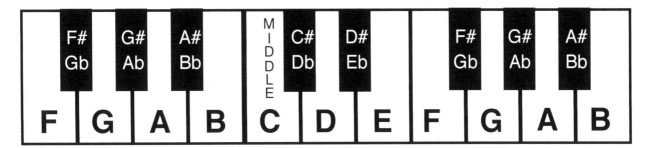

- You might have noticed in the last two lessons that there are 2 names for each Black Key: A Sharp Name and a Flat Name. This is true for the entire piano.
- Depending on the musical context (which we will learn more about throughout this book), a black key may be called by either its sharp or flat name. For example, A Flat and G Sharp are the same key on the piano; C Sharp and D Flat are the same key; and F Sharp and G Flat are the same key. See Above.

Scarborough Fair

- *Scarborough Fair* is in 3/4 Time. Count: One, Two, Three
- For the F#, play the black key directly to the right of F on the piano.

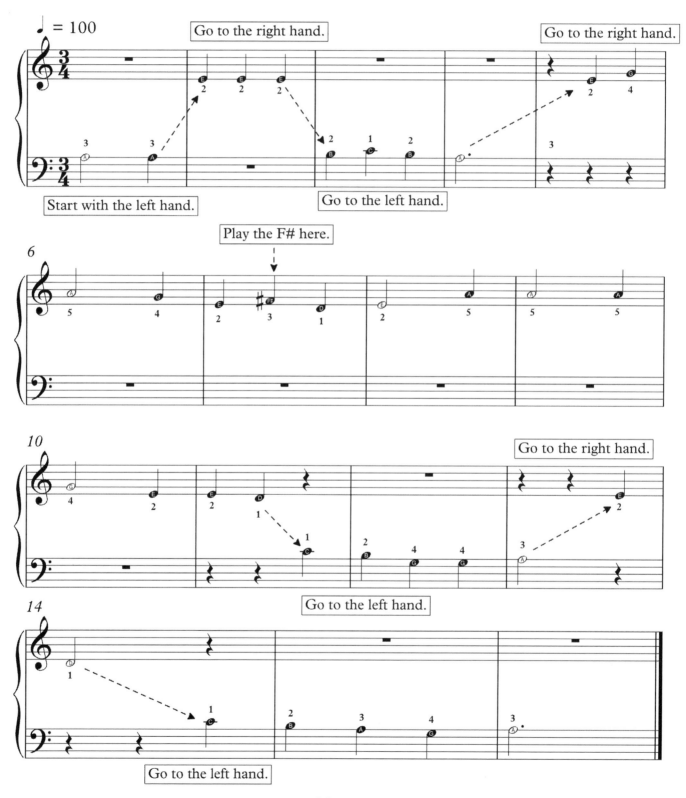

Easy Chords Overview:
C Major, F Major & G7

Check out video 12

- Chords are 3 or more notes played at the same time.
- In order to play chords well, keep your fingers curved for the notes that you play and lift your fingers that are not being used for the chord.
- Take a look at video lesson 16 to see and hear how these techniques work.
- For these chords, use the Left Hand (LH).
- We are going to look at 3 chords in this lesson.

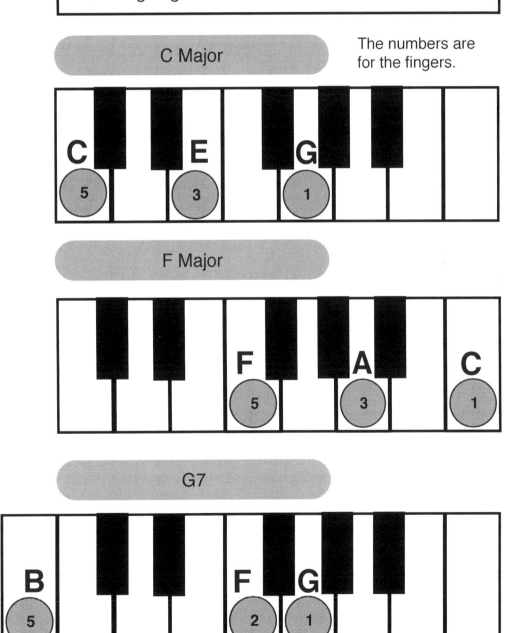

The numbers are for the fingers.

More Easy Chords
A Minor, D Minor & G

- Let's look at 3 more chords for the Left Hand: A Minor, D Minor, & G Major.
- Make sure to keep your fingers curved and lift the fingers that do not play.
- Listen to the difference in sound between the major and minor chords.

The numbers are for the fingers.

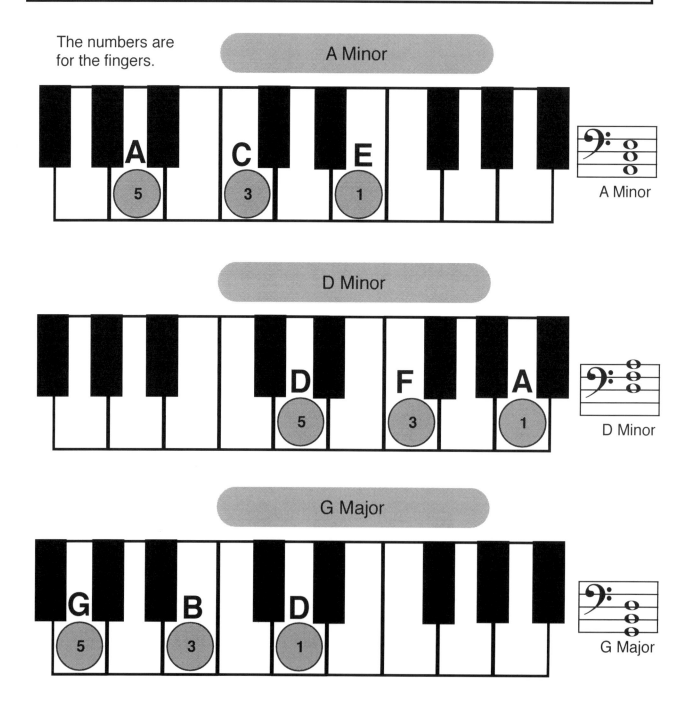

Chord Overview & Exercise

In this lesson, we are going to practice playing some of the chords from the previous two lessons. With each of these exercises, take your time to master the transition from one chord to the next. Building up this kind of left-hand coordination will greatly help you, once we start learning the songs with left-hand chords from the next section of the book. If you have a metronome, you might set it to quarter note equals 60 (in other words sixty beats per minute) for this exercise. As a side note, there are many free metronome apps available online. If you have a smart phone, tablet, computer, or similar electronic device, you might take a moment to find a free metronome app for it online; you can use a metronome to help you learn the pieces later in the book.

When you move from one chord to the next, try to form the new chord with your fingers, before playing the keys. This technique will improve your muscle memory for the chords. Along these lines, try to avoid sliding your fingers along the keyboard to find the notes of the chords. This will not only hamper the development of your muscle memory for playing chords, but it will also make it more likely that you will play a few wrong notes.

Chord Dance:
C Major & G7 Chords

- *Chord Dance* is in 4/4 Time. There are 4 beats per measure.
- The song has C Major and G7 chords.

Red River Valley

Focus mainly on the right-hand melody.
The chords are fairly simple.

The Gs have a tie.
Hold for 3 beats.

From this val - ley they say you are go ing.__ I will miss your bright

eyes and sweet smile. For they say you are tak - ing the sun- shine

that has bright - ened our path - way a - while.

Aura Lee

Ode to Joy,
Chord Version

Check out video 13

- This version of *Ode to Joy* uses the C Major and G7 Chords.
- Remember to count the beats as you play.
- The piece is in 4/4 Time: 4 Beats per measure.

Ode to Joy

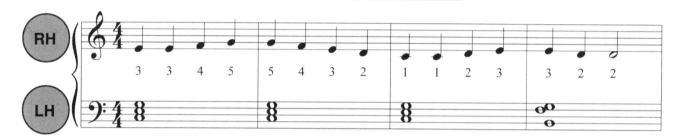

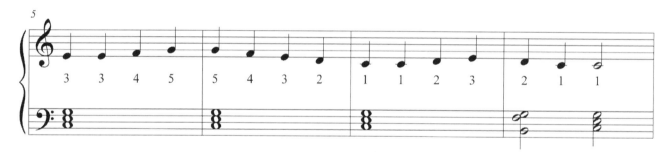

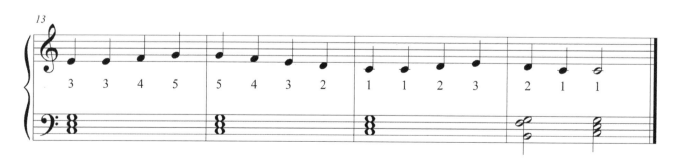

Jazz Dance

- *Jazz Dance* is in 4/4 Time (4 Beats per Measure).
- The melody has quarter notes and half notes.
- The chords are in the left hand.
- The melody is in the right hand.
- Play the chords on the first beat of each measure.

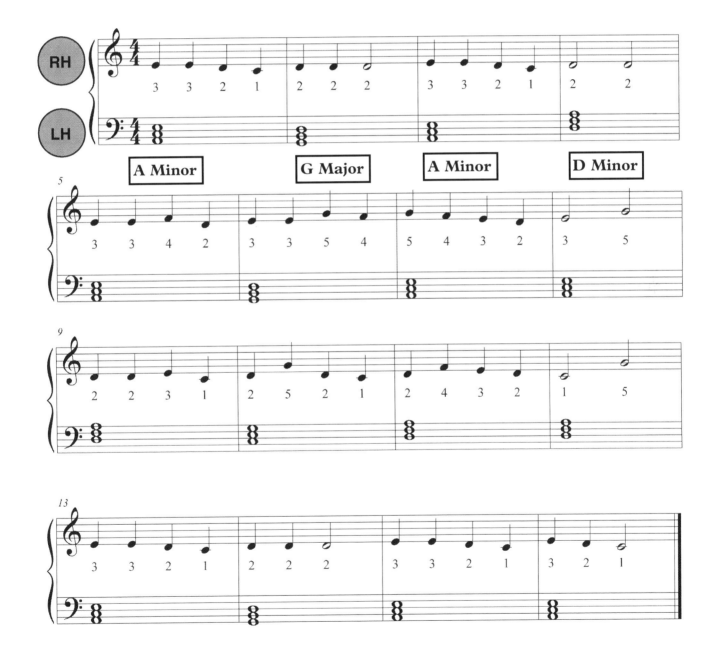

House of the Rising Sun

The first RH Position is A, B, C, D, E: 1, 2, 3, 4, 5

These are the chord names.

We are in 3/4 Time. Count "1, 2, 3" for each measure.

There is a house in

This is an upbeat. Start on beat 3.

We will use the same fingering for each chord in this song: 5, 3, 1 with the left hand.

New Or - leans they

The D Major chord has an F# with the third finger.

Jump up an octave with your 5th finger (pinky). The new RH Position is D, E, F, G, A.

call the ris - - ing

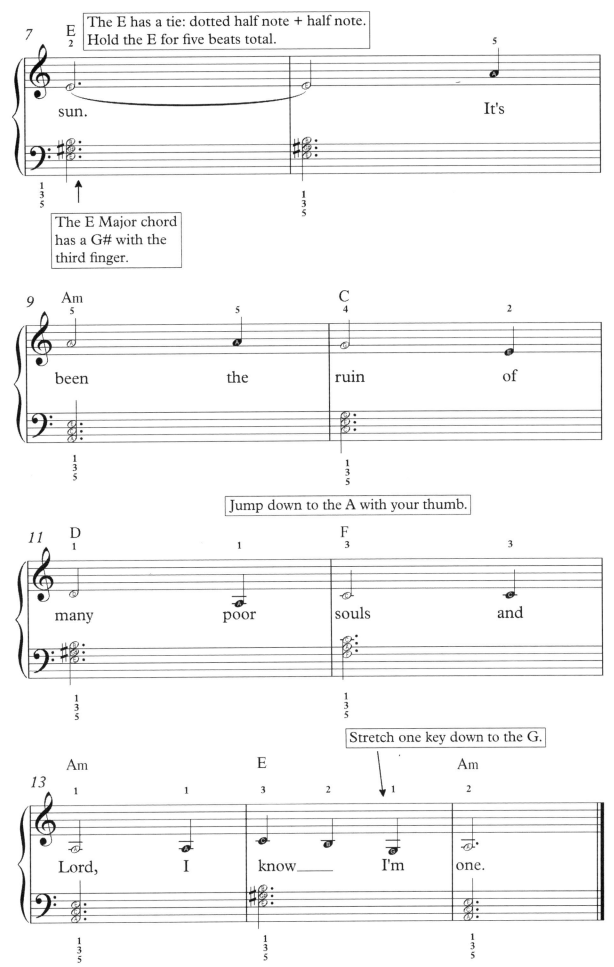

Music Theory: Overview of Dynamics

As we continue, let's look at a few music concepts that come up in some songs and pieces of music.

Dynamics is a term that we use for the loudness and softness of the notes in music. In pieces and songs you will see dynamic indications represented as letters (F, P, MP, or MF, for example). These letters are abbreviations for Italian words.

p stands for the term "piano", which means soft (like a whisper, but not the quietest whisper).

mp stands for the term "mezzo-piano", which means medium soft (like a quiet conversation).

mf stands for the term "mezzo-forte", which means medium loud (like a normal conversation).

f stands for the term "forte", which means loud (like a shout).

Dynamics are a relative concept in music. In other words, you might consider that each piece has a slightly different range from soft to loud. Forte ("loud") in the context of a Beethoven piece may be a little different than forte in a Mozart piece. So, let's think of dynamics as a general concept that vary slightly from piece to piece. Part of what makes music so exciting and inspiring is finding the nuance and detail in the poetics of each piece. Exploring dynamics on the piano, along with many other musical concepts will be a big part of this book.

In piano sheet music (sometimes called the "score"), we are given indications on how to make the music gradually louder or softer. In a lighthearted way, you might think of this as the piano version of turning up or turning down the volume on a car stereo, TV, or an audio device. In piano music we use two symbols:

Crescendo means to get gradually louder

Diminuendo means to get gradually quieter

Simple Gifts Overview & Lesson

Let's look again at *Simple Gifts.* This is the wonderful Americana theme that inspired Aaron Copland in his famous piece, *Appalachian Spring.* The theme has a dancelike character, which is energized by the use of eighth notes in the melody. Eighth notes are equal to half of a quarter note and are counted as half of a beat.

They look like this:

In a measure of 4/4 time, eight eighth notes would be counted counted like this: 1 &, 2 &, 3 &, 4 &. The "&" stands for the word "and". The "&" or "and" is the halfway point of a beat. See the example below:

Musicians often refer to the halfway point of a beat as the "and". For example, a musician might say, "play it on the *and* of *two*". This would mean: play it at the halfway point of beats two and three.

When you divide a beat into sections, it is called "subdividing". Let's practice counting and playing groups of eighth notes and quarter notes. Remember to subdivide the eighth notes: for example, 1 &, 2 &, 3 &, 4 &.

In exercise one, we discover that the melody is exchanged between the left and right hands. The melody starts in the left hand and then moves to the right hand. Also, the first note is an upbeat or pickup note. This is a device that helps emphasize part of a musical phrase. The first note (G) leans into the second note (middle C). The G will be on the fourth beat of the measure. So, count: 1, 2, 3, 4. On beat four, play the G. Then go into the next measure, the first full measure, and play middle C on the downbeat (beat one).

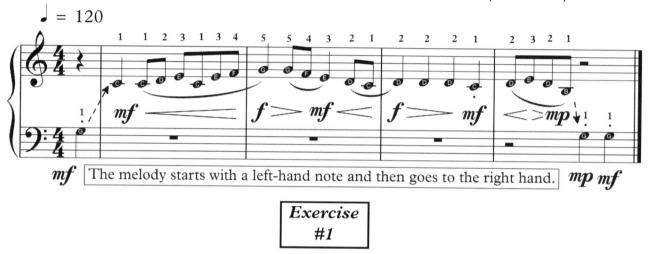

Exercise
#1

In piano music, phrases (the musical equivalent of sentences in language) are indicated by the use of slurs (or phrase markers). Slurs are curved lines that go over or under two or more different notes. When you finish a phrase in music, you should lift your hand or fingers a little bit to separate it from the next phrase. Slurs also indicate to play in a smooth (*legato*) manner on the piano. You can see some slurs in the melody for *Simple Gifts*.

Exercise
#2

Let's now practice the melody in the left hand, as exercise two. Start this exercise slowly and then gradually build up the speed. Make sure that you pay special attention to the finger numbers; there are a few little shifts.

Simple Gifts

Remember to subdivide for the eighth notes.

Practice the left-hand chords alone, until they are comfortable, before playing with both hands .

The note names are listed inside each note.

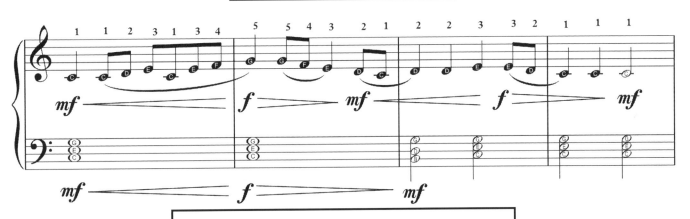

The dynamic marks indicate how loud or soft to play the piece. They also indicate whether the music should get gradually louder or softer.

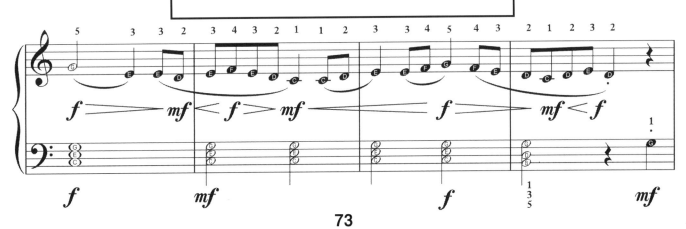

The melody moves between hands here.

Practice the right-hand chords alone, until they are comfortable, before playing with both hands .

Pay attention to the finger numbers in the left hand.

We have four new chords for *Happy Birdthday:*

G in First Inversion:
the note B is in the bass.
Use fingers 5, 3, 1.

F in First Inversion:
the note A is in the bass.
Use fingers 5, 3, 1.

F in Second Inversion:
the note C is in the bass.
Use fingers 5, 2, 1

Bb
Major
Use fingers 5, 3, 1

Happy Birthday

These letters are
the chord names.

The note names are
inside the notes.

The curved line is a tie:
Hold the E for 6 beats.

Lesson on Brahms' Lullaby

Let's look at this famous lullaby by Johannes Brahms. In exercise one, we are going to focus on the left hand. This left-hand chord style of alternating a bass note with a small chord is a very common technique in piano playing. Some people refer to it as the "um, pa, pa" style, since it simulates the sound of an orchestra or band playing the accompaniment (or background music) for a melody. When playing this "um, pa, pa" style, lean your hand and wrist down slightly and to the left a little bit to emphasize the first note of the measure; in measure one, this would be low note C. Then, slightly lift your hand back to its regular position for the second two beats; for the first measures, this would be the chords with the notes E and G. Follow this same motion for the entire piece. Count 1, 2, 3 for each measure.

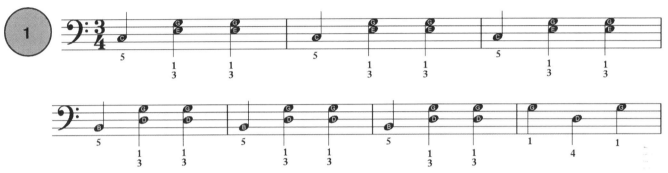

In exercise two, let's look at the beginning melody of the piece. The music is in 3/4 time signature. This means that there will be three beats in a measure and that the quarter note will get the beat. Also, the first measure is an upbeat. An upbeat is a note or set of notes that push into the downbeat (the first beat of the next measure). You might think of the phrase "the end", where the word "the" is accented to emphasize the word "end". Try saying it emphasizing the word "the": **The** end. A similar effect takes place for the two E notes that begin the melody. They are slightly accented to "push" into the G, which is the third note of the melody. Count: 1, 2, 3. On the count of three, play the upbeat E. This upbeat figure occurs several times in the lullaby.

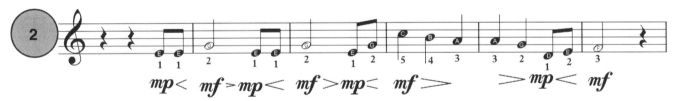

For exercise three, let's put both hands together. Try this slowly and then gradually build up the speed to a moderate tempo. Remember to count to three (1,2, 3) for each measure. Also, remember the upbeat figure at the beginning.

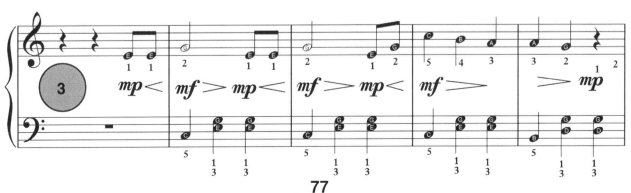

Lullaby

Check out video 14

Johannes Brahms

Shenandoah & Hineh Ma Tov in Um-Pah Chord Style

Shenandoah

Hineh Ma Tov

This lyrical piece is in a minor key: A Minor. Listen for the difference in sound quality.

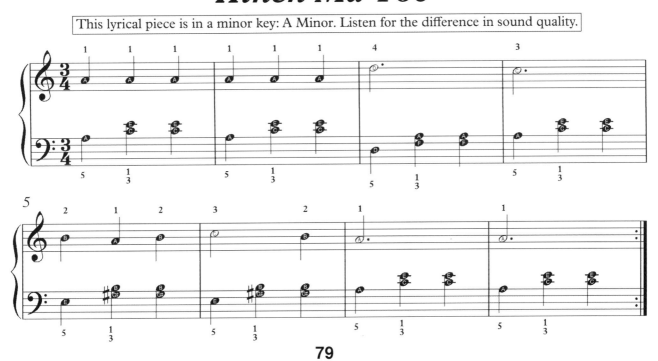

Home on the Range

This Little Light of Mine

81

Greensleeves Lesson & Overview

In exercise one, we are going to look at the left-hand technique for *Greensleeves*. Most of the left-hand sections outline chords, played one note at a time. These are called "arpeggios" in music terminology. The word "arpeggio" is Italian and means harp. So, when you are playing this preliminary exercise, try to imagine the piano sounding a little bit like a harp. If possible, let your left-hand wrist drop down a little bit at the beginning of each measure. At the end of each measure, let it raise back to its normal position: parallel to the left hand.

In exercise two, we are gong to focus on the rhythm for the melody in the right hand. We are going to exclude all of the notes of the melody, except for "D". As you take a look a the rhythm for the melody of *Greensleeves,* you will notice that it is in 3/4 time (that is, three quarter notes or their equivalent in each measure) and composed of half notes, quarter notes, eighth notes, and dotted-quarter notes. The dotted quarter notes are equal to one and a half beats. You should count them like this: 1&2. Take a moment to find the note "D" with your right hand thumb and try the exercise. Remember to count the beats and subdivisions (the sections marked between each beat).

Now, in exercise three, let's try playing the right-hand melody of the opening. Please use (and even memorize) the fingering that is listed. As a general guideline, it's best to always strive to use the same fingering once you learn a piece of music. This way, your mind will not have to constantly be figuring out which fingers to place on the keys.

In exercise four, let's take a look at another section of the melody in the right hand. You might notice that the index finger will move over the thumb in measure two. As well, please notice the dynamics: forte down to mezzopiano. This means that it will go from loud (relative to the overall sound of the piece) down to fairly soft. When you are playing the piece, starting on the next page, try to make the right hand a little bit louder than the left. This will balance the sound of the piece and bring out the melody.

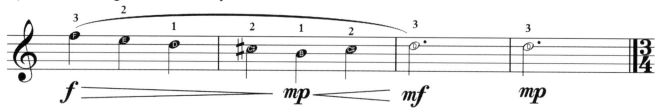

Greensleeves

Play the left-hand part softer
than the right-hand part.

J.S. Bach Prelude in C Major Overview & Arpeggios

In this lesson, we are going to prepare for playing the *C Major Prelude* by J.S. Bach. Arpeggios are one of the key concepts at work in this piece. The term "arpeggio" comes from the Italian word "arpa", which means "harp". Along these lines, an arpeggio is a chord played one note at a time, instead of a chord where all of the notes are played at once. This style of playing one note at a time mimics the sound of a harp.

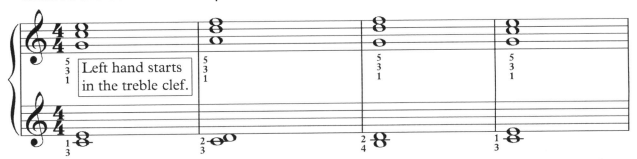

Let's start by playing the first eight measures as chords, rather than arpeggios. This method of reducing the arpeggios to block chords can be done for the entire piece and will make it easier to learn.

Once you are comfortable with the fingering, try playing the first four measures as arpeggios (one note at a time).

Prelude in C Major

Check out video 15

Adagio · Try to bring out the top note of each measure.

J.S. Bach

Left hand starts in the treble clef.

This measure has the same fingering as the previous one. This two-measure pattern occurs for the whole piece.

These two measures are the same as the first two in the piece. They act as a kind of "little ending", before the music moves in a different harmonic direction.

These are high A notes.

The F# repeats in this measure.

The F# repeats in this measure too.

This is the B
below middle C.

The F# repeats
in this measure.

This is the A
below middle C.

This is the A
below middle C.

The left hand will go into
the bass clef in this measure.

Slow down a little bit in the last two measues.
This will indicate that the piece is ending.

87

Music Theory: What is a Scale?

- Scales are groups of notes that are arranged in stepwise patterns, either going up or going down. The combination of these steps (also called "Intervals") gives each type of scale its unique sound and character.

- Most scales are made up of Half Steps and Whole Steps.

- A Half Step (also called "Minor Second" Interval) is the distance from one piano key to the very next piano key, for example, from C to C# (white key to black key) or from E to F. In both cases, there are no keys (whether white keys or black keys) between those two notes.

- Whole Steps (also called "Major Second" Intervals), are made up of two Half Steps. For example, C to D is a whole step: 2 Half Steps combined--C to C# and then C# to D. See the Chart Below.

Half Half
Step Step

Check out video 16

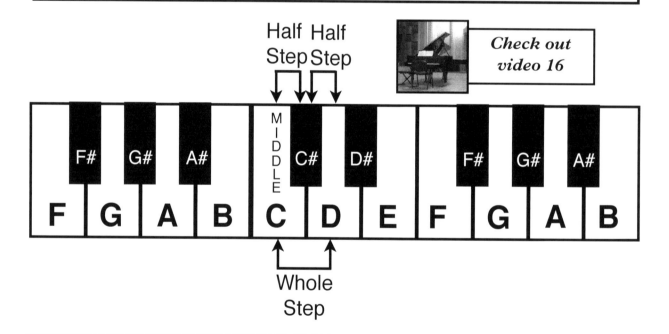

Whole
Step

- Here are some other examples of Whole Steps: G to A, E to D, B to C#, F to G.
- Try playing the following Whole Steps (going up or down) and listen to their sound characteristics: A to B, C# to D#, A to G, F# to G#. Use the chart above to help you locate the notes. Listen to the similarities between each group.

Music Theory
What is a Major Scale?

- All Major Scales follow the same pattern of whole steps and half steps.

- All Major Scales have 8 notes. For example, here are the notes of the C Major Scale: C, D, E, F, G, A, B, C. There are 8 notes (or keys) total.

- The Pattern for all Major Scales, Ascending (going up on the keyboard), is: 2 Whole Steps, 1 Half Step, 3 Whole Steps, then 1 Half Step.

- In the 2 diagrams below, take a look at the pattern of Whole Steps and Half Steps. Try playing the C Major Scale (shown below) and listen to the steps.

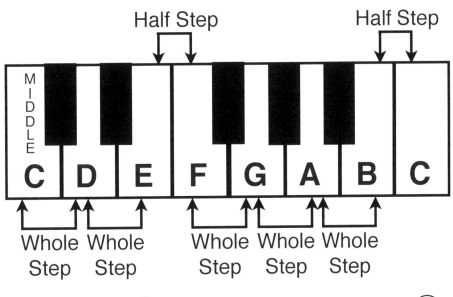

Whole Step = Ⓦ   Half Step = Ⓗ

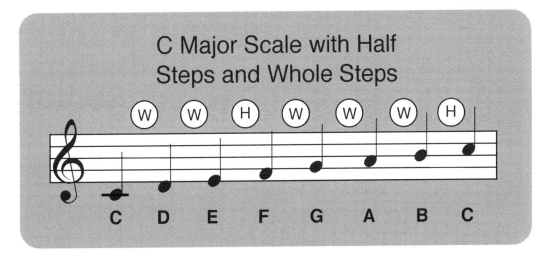

C Major Scale with Half Steps and Whole Steps

Five-Finger Scales (RH)
C, G, and D Major

• In these 3 exercises, we will be playing the first 5 notes of the C, D, and G Major Scales in the Right Hand. Remember to keep your fingers curved as you play. After you practice these patterns 10 times. **Have Fun!**

C Major

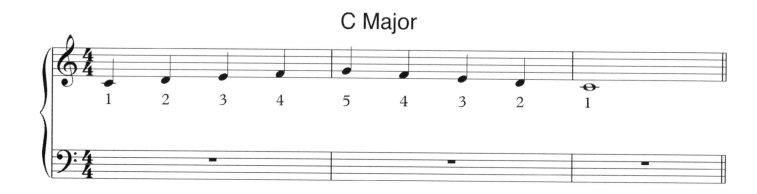

G Major

The Sharps are added here to help.

D Major

Five-Finger Scales (LH)
C, G, and D Major

> • In these 3 exercises, we will be playing the first 5 notes of the C, D, and G Major Scales in the Left Hand. Remember to keep your fingers curved as you play. After you practice these patterns 10 times. **Have Fun!**

C Major

G Major

The Sharps are added here to help.

D Major

Five-Finger Scales (Both Hands) C, G, and D Major

- In these 3 exercises, we will be playing the first 5 notes of the C, D, and G Major Scales in Both Hands. Remember to keep your fingers curved as you play.

- In our next piece, we will look at *The New World Symphony Theme.* This beautiful melody uses elements of the major scale. ***Enjoy!***

C Major

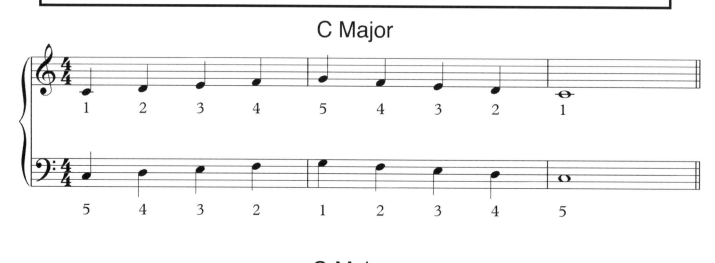

G Major

The Sharps are added here to help.

D Major

Lesson on New World Symphony Theme & How to Play Dotted Rhythms

In Dvorak's *Theme from the New World Symphony*, we have a few new musical concepts. The first one is syncopation. Syncopation is when notes occur on weaker beats or between beats. The strongest beat in every measure is beat one, which is called the "downbeat" of the measure. In 4/4 time, beat three is the second strongest beat.

When notes occur between beats, we have to use a technique called subdividing to count the rhythm. We talked about subdividing for our lesson on *Simple Gifts,* as well. Subdividing means that we are going to cut the beats into smaller sections. The simplest of these subdivisions is to cut each beat in half. In music, we use the word "and" and the symbol "&" for the halfway point between each beat. For example, if we have a measure of 4/4 time, where we want to subdivide each beat in half we would count: "1 & 2 & 3 & 4 &". Try counting it aloud. The eighth notes (notes with a flag or beam) count as half of a beat. In other words, two eighth notes equal one quarter note. Just to refresh your memory, this is what an eighth note looks like:

In exercise one, we have two rhythms for the melody of the piece. Try counting these out loud, while playing the rhythms on middle C.

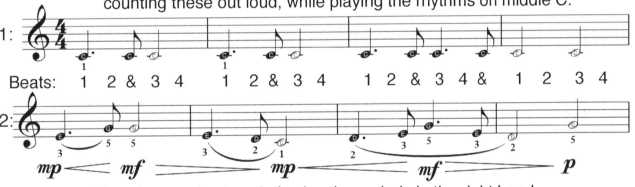

Now, in exercise two, let's play the melody in the right hand.

Each chord or note (in LH) will occur on a beat. For each measure, count: 1, 2, 3, 4.

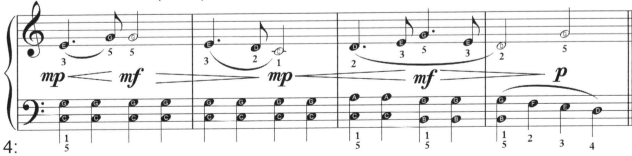

Now, let's put both hands together for exercise four. Listen to how the right hand is syncopated against the left hand. Remember to subdivide while you are counting.

93

New World Symphony Theme

Antonín Dvořák

Silent Night

For *Silent Night*, there are several position changes in the right hand. Pay close attention to the finger numbers.

Turkish Rondo

Check out video 17, which has more
information on playing scale passages.

Wolfgang Amadeus Mozart

The piece uses small sections ("phrases") of scales.

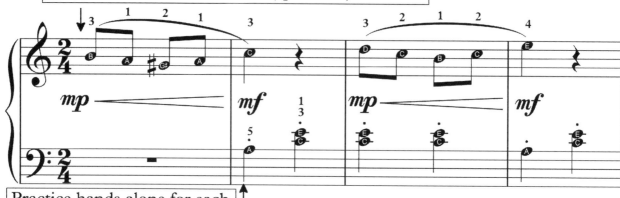

Practice hands alone for each
line ("system") of music, then
put both hands together.

There is an "Um Pah" style in the left hand.

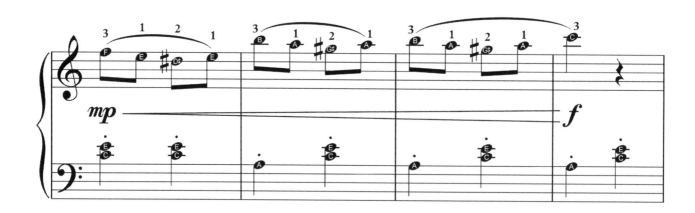

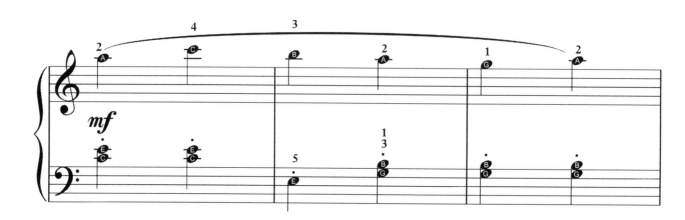

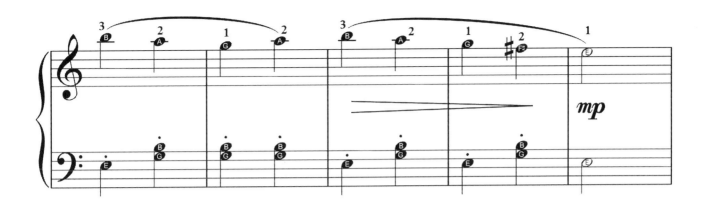

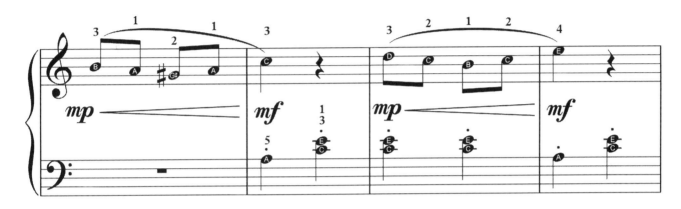

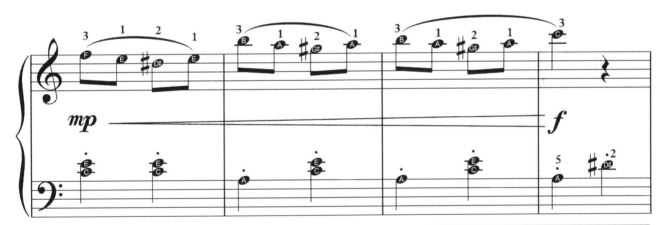

This rhythm is a triplet: three notes per beat.
For the measure, count "1 &" for the first beat.
For the second beat, count: "2, 2, 3".

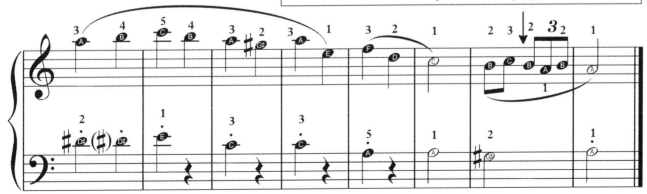

Lesson & Overview on Grieg's Hall of the Mountain King

Hall of the Mountain King is a fun and energetic piece to play.

In exercise one, we are going to practice the Alberti bass figures for the left hand. Please notice that the position changes in the fourth measure. There is a new symbol in this piece: *8vb*. This symbol and the bracket that follows it indicates that we should play one octave (eight notes) lower than what is written. There is a corresponding symbol: *8va*. When you see this symbol, play an octave (eight notes) higher than written.

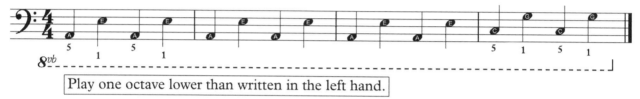

Play one octave lower than written in the left hand.

We will now move to the right hand, for exercise two. Please note that the piece starts in the bass clef for the right hand and gradually rises up into the treble clef for the left hand. For the first two and a half measures, we will stay in a position around the notes A, B, C, D, and E. Halfway through measure three, we will change to a new position. This right hand pattern will repeat throughout the piece.

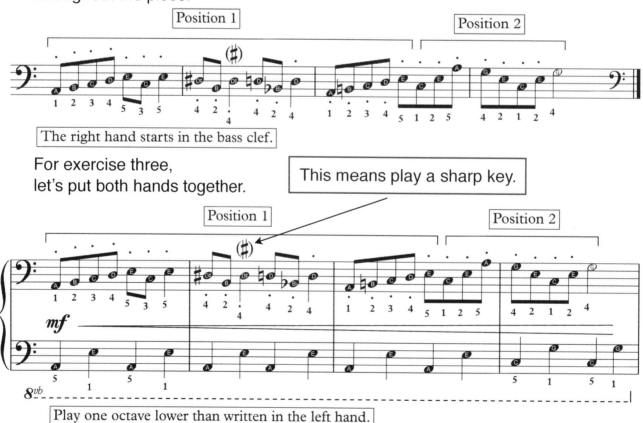

The right hand starts in the bass clef.

For exercise three, let's put both hands together.

This means play a sharp key.

Play one octave lower than written in the left hand.

98

In exercise four, let's practice this melody for the right hand. The first five notes of the melody fit comfortably under the hand; you will play part of an ascending (going up) A Minor scale (the notes A, B, C, D, and E). On the sixth note of the melody, your hand will change positions and your fingers will need to spread out a little bit more. Also notice that the dynamics go from mezzo-forte (medium loud) to forte (loud). Try to play this melody in a smooth, legato manner, as opposed to the staccato (bouncy) style for the right hand in the previous exercise.

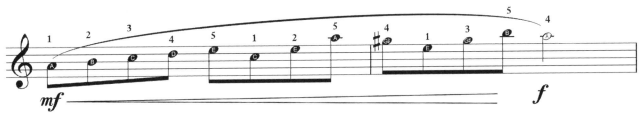

The first two measures of exercise five have dissonant ("spicy" or "agitated") chords. We also have accents (>) over the chords. Accents give a sudden jolt of energy to the music. In the left hand, you will play the notes C, Eb, and Gb for the chord. Try playing each measure of this exercise hands alone. Then put both hands together for each measure. Finally, play the whole exercise with both hands.

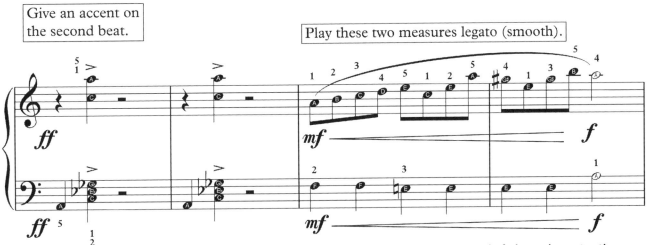

Exercise six starts with a long, A Minor scale that goes from the left hand up to the right hand. On the sixth note of the scale, the third finger of your left hand will need to go over your thumb. In the second measure, the scale will continue in the right hand. Practice this exercise slowly to build up your coordination.

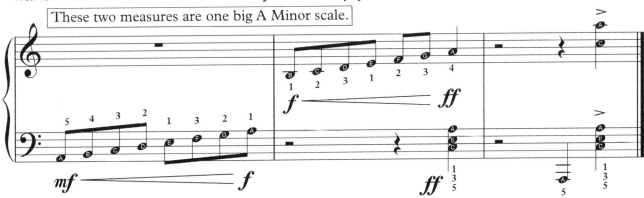

Hall of the Mountain King

Check out video 18 for information on minor scales.

The right hand starts in the bass clef.

Listen for the repeated patterns throughout the piece.

Play one octave lower than written in the left hand.

Play one octave higher than written in the right hand.

Play one octave lower than written in the left hand.

Change to treble clef.

Play one octave lower than written in the left hand.

Play one octave lower than written in the left hand.

Canon

Check out video 19

We are now going to combine scales and arpeggios for this wonderful piece. Take your time and play hands alone for each measure. Then, play with both hands together for the measure, before going to the next measure.

Adagio

Johann Pachelbel

For the first four measures, the right hand is one octave (eight notes) higher than written.

Go from the left hand to the right hand.

The left hand starts in the treble clef.

102

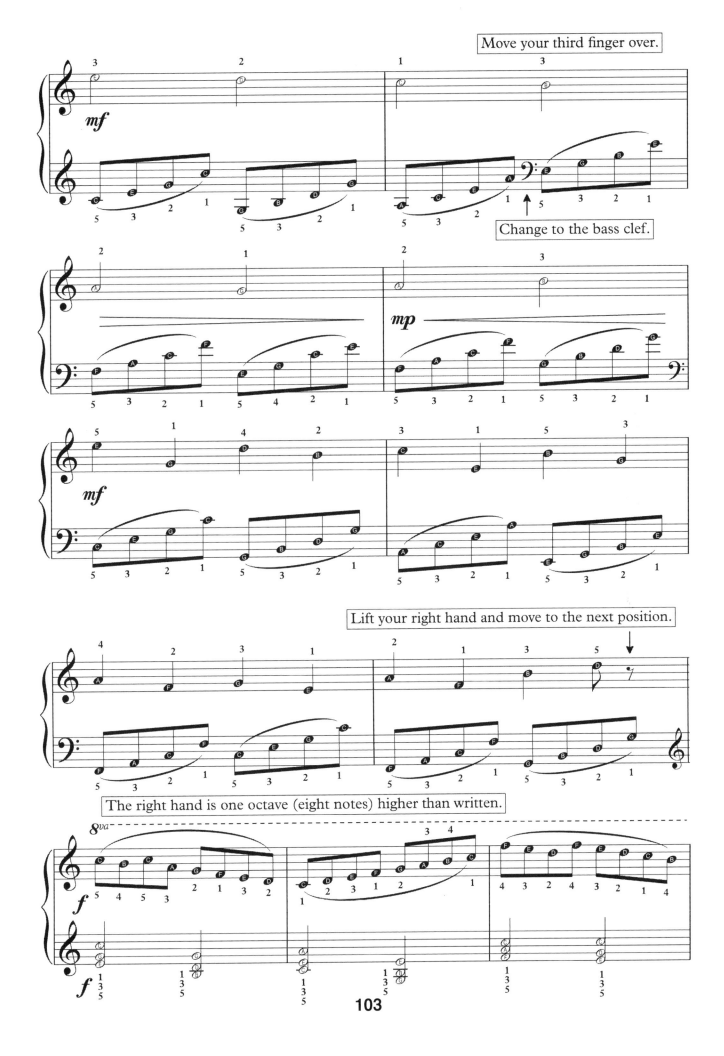

Move your third finger over.

Change to the bass clef.

Lift your right hand and move to the next position.

The right hand is one octave (eight notes) higher than written.

103

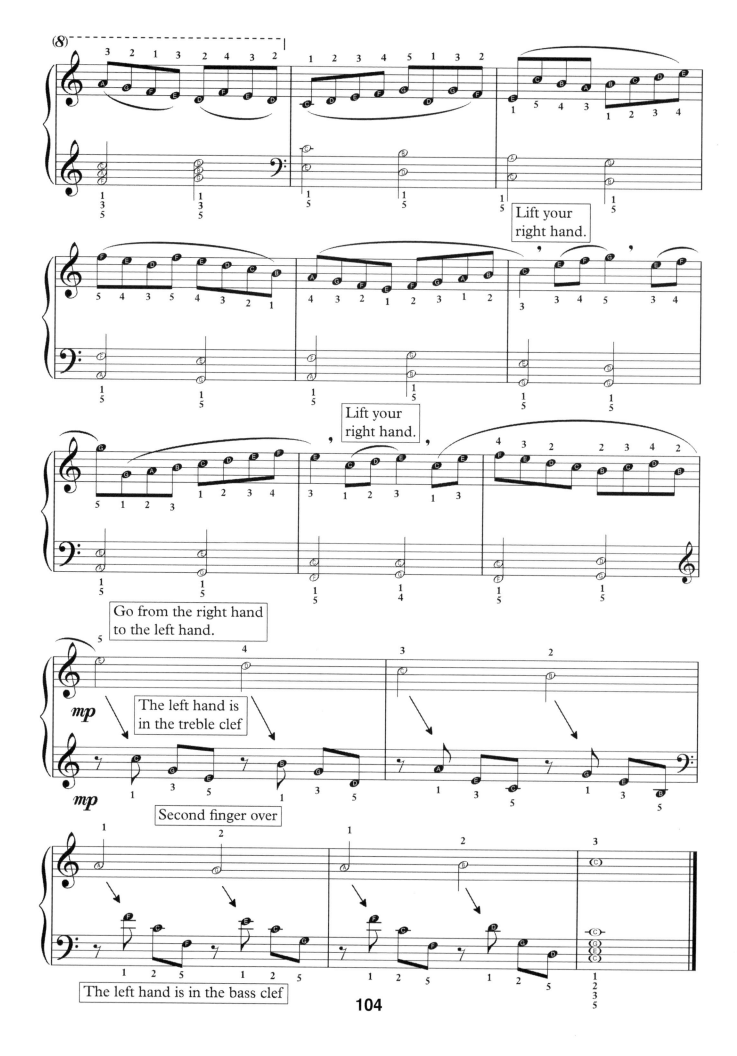

Lift your right hand.

Lift your right hand.

Go from the right hand to the left hand.

The left hand is in the treble clef

Second finger over

The left hand is in the bass clef

104

The Entertainer

The piece starts with an upbeat. Count: 1, 2, 3, 4 &. Start on "4 &".

Play one hand at a time for each line. Pay close attention to the finger numbers and remember to count.

There are several position changes for each hand throughout the piece.

Scott Joplin

Practice the left hand first. It will act like the conductor: keeping a steady, regular beat.

The dots indicate staccato notes: bouncy.

The second finger goes over the thumb in this measure.

Pay attention to any patterns in the melody.

These three measures are the same as the first system.

Pay close attention to the tied notes.

In this system, focus on the left hand. The right hand mainly plays three notes: C, D & E.

The left-hand bass notes go down by step.

105

Für Elise

Ludwig van Beethoven

For the E's in these two measures, play: Left, Left, Left, Right, Right, Left, Left, Right, Right.

For the D#'s and E's in these two measures, play: Left, Left, Right, Right, Left, Left, Right, Right, Right.

Second finger over.

Alternate hands.

Left hand in the treble clef

Second finger over.

Congratulations!
You have completed the Book!

Great work in completing this book and video course on the basics of piano. You now have an understanding of the fundamentals of piano playing: basic piano technique, beginner-level note reading and chord playing, a repertoire of songs and pieces to perform for family and friends, and some understanding of music fundamentals--such as time signatures, beats, and the grand staff.

To continue to the next level, I would suggest two book and video courses:

1. *Beginner Classical Piano Music*
2. *Piano Scales, Chords & Arpeggio Lessons with Basic Music Theory*

Keep up the good work and continue to practice and play the piano!

Damon Ferrante

If you enjoyed this book, please recommend the paperback edition to your local library.

Damon Ferrante is a composer, guitarist, and professor of piano studies. He has taught on the music faculties of Seton Hall University and Montclair State University. For over 20 years, Damon has taught guitar, piano, composition, and music theory. Damon has had performances at Carnegie Hall, Symphony Space, and throughout the US and Europe. His main teachers have been David Rakowski at Columbia University, Stanley Wolfe at Juilliard, and Bruno Amato at the Peabody Conservatory of Johns Hopkins University. Damon has written two operas, a guitar concerto, song cycles, orchestral music, and numerous solo and chamber music works. He has over 30 music books and scores in print. For more information on his books, concerts, and music, please visit steeplechasearts.com.

Two More Best-Selling Piano Books by Damon Ferrante!

Beginner Classical Piano Music

Teach Yourself How to Play Famous Piano Pieces by Bach, Mozart, Beethoven & the Great Composers

Includes Streaming Videos!

Damon Ferrante

Book, Streaming Videos & MP3 Audio

Piano Scales Chords
Arpeggios Lessons

Book & Videos   Damon Ferrante

Made in United States
Orlando, FL
31 July 2022

20408906R00067